FELLINI LEXICON

This

FELLINI LEXICON

Sam Rohdie

bfi Publishing

For Bill Routt

First published in 2002 by the
British Film Institute
21 Stephen Street, London W1P 2LN

The British Film Institute promotes greater understanding of,
and access to, film and moving image culture in the UK.

Cover design: Paul Wright/Cube
Cover images: *Roma*; *Notti di Cabiria*
Set in Italian Garamond by ketchup, London
Printed in England by The Cromwell Press, Trowbridge

British Library Cataloguing-in-Publication Data
A catalogue record for this book is available from the British Library
ISBN 0 85170 934-6 pbk
ISBN 0 85170 933-8 hbk

Contents

Acknowledgments

I want to especially thank Zygmunt Baranski, Bill Routt and my editor Rob White.

Des O'Rawe helped me enormously in substance and in spirit.

I am grateful for the help of Patricia McMurray, Geoffrey Nowell-Smith and Peter Stambler.

As ever there was Lam Shuk Foon with her love, patience, curiosity, charm, gaiety, wit, silliness, joy, smiles and a giggle in her eyes … my Cabiria.

Introduction

I decided to write this book as a lexicon, following a set of procedures. The procedures impose limits among which are brevity, precision, exactness.

The rules of the lexicon are:
- there is no order of reading or writing save the alphabetical (the arbitrary);
- entries are about function;
- entries are brief;
- there is no attempt at comprehensiveness.

I have made choices in accord with what I believe to be structurally pertinent to Fellini's films. The choices are also matters of chance, preference and association. An entry 'conmen' can lead to 'angels', or 'clowns', and also to 'trumpets'.

The lexicon is not scholarly nor scientific.
It is a play with meanings rather than their definition.
Fellini's films lend themselves to affiliation, overlap, superimposition.

I do not delimit what Fellini thinks, but try instead to specify how his films work. An idea, a theme, characters, settings in his films, belong to a web of intricate relations. It is the processes of the formation of those relations that interests me.
Each entry further weaves the web.
The entries in the lexicon are points of adhesion and also dispersion, condensing, then spinning out.

Unless otherwise indicated all quotes in French and Italian are from Fellini texts cited in the bibliography; translations are my own except where the original quote from Fellini is in English.

Angels

Strictly speaking, there are no angels in Fellini's films. No character represents an angel.

Some characters resemble angels or do angelic things.

Such likenesses appear casually as if by accident, as a matter of association. You discover an analogy, a mirroring, catching it.

The Fellinian angel is born of metaphor.

The peasants with faggots on their backs who pass Augusto in *Il bidone* as he lays dying beside the road are nothing out of the ordinary, nothing other than they are, peasants with faggots on their backs belonging to reality, to this world, yet the faggots look like wings and as a consequence the peasants, angels.

Otto e mezzo: 'Claudia'

The faggot on Gelsomina's back in *La strada* as she is called from the beach is a fact of reality. Yet, by a shift in view, it transports her to another world.

Her mother sells her to Zampanò. At that moment Gelsomina finds another existence imagining being elsewhere. She will journey with Zampanò into the world. The world to her is magic, make-believe, theatre, masquerade, spectacle, clowning. Gelsomina is overjoyed. She accomplishes the journey in her imagination and anticipation before it begins.

This imagination is angelic.

Picasso saw in two metal toy cars, placed bottom to bottom, the head of a baboon; in everyday nails, he saw the feet of a chicken; in bicycle handlebars, the horns of a bull; in scraps of wood and paper, a guitar.

There was nothing symbolic in these transformative sights.

The toy cars remain what they are (toy cars) to become what they are not (the head of a baboon) which they could be (in sculpture) if only you can see the likeness, the poetry in the banal, the fantastic in the quotidian.

Such strategies are not representational.

The toy cars do not represent the head of a baboon. They are the head of a baboon. And they are not.

There can be a make-believe without falsity, a make-believe *with* reality.

By such means the world is expanded.

Nothing changes yet every object, every moment is opened to an infinity of relations and possibilities by remaining what it is in order to be truly itself, and not. The universe becomes filled with unlikely paradigms.

As a result, vast distances can be traversed.

In *La strada*, 'Il matto' on the high wire, has wings attached to his back. To Gelsomina he seems an angel. When 'Il matto' descends the wire he notices Gelsomina. She seems to him to be an angel in the guise of a clown as he to her is a clown in the guise of an angel.

Her clown aspect (and his) are matters of resemblance, suggestions only. Resemblance makes them a couple. Angels, clowns, actors belong to otherworldliness, to the fantastic. You have to be a bit mad, certainly fanciful, to follow the lines of suggestion, perhaps you need to be an angel yourself.

Angels exist in Fellinian reality but they require our imagination to summon them into being.

Marcello in *La dolce vita* says to the young girl, Paola, in the restaurant by the beach: 'You look like an angel in an Umbrian church.'

In that instant she is an angel and remains herself.

The sadness of *La dolce vita* is that Marcello by the end of the film can neither recognise the young girl as herself nor as an angel in an Umbrian church.

He has lost sight.

The loss of sight is a loss of hope and thereby of invention, possibility, imagination, the loss of metaphor, the renunciation of the invisible. Joy has left the world for Marcello after having seen death and despair in the infanticide and suicide of Steiner where he also saw a part of himself and a part thereby of everyone.

Fausto and Moraldo in *I vitelloni* steal the statue of an angel from Fausto's employer, a seller of religious articles who has fired Fausto. Fausto and Moraldo wrap the statue in a cloth and put it on a handcart. Accompanied by the town's lunatic they bring the statue to a monastery where they try unsuccessfully to sell it. The friar, who refuses them, is perched on the branch of a tree (like an angel).

Fausto and Moraldo try to sell the statue at a convent to a nun, who is fragile and innocent, like Marcello's angel.

The friar and the nun are beings from another world while remaining in this one.

Dejected, the dishonest trio sprawl on vacant land, the statue of the angel beside them. Could they be the three Magi dressed as clowns? Or the Holy Trinity?

The lunatic is overtaken with joy. He sees an angel in the statue. The sight is not secular, not an angel represented, but spiritual, an angel present. An angel is there though nothing has changed, only a perspective.

This moment is like a miracle.

Reality is transformed without anything having happened.

The wife of the owner of the religious articles shop where Fausto works is plain, ordinary, dull. She is the provincial wife of a provincial shopkeeper. It is the eve of New Year. There is a celebration for the entire town. Fausto brings his new wife Sandrina to the celebration. The shopkeeper brings his wife. The wife enters the spectacle of the celebration and begins to glow, to scintillate like fireworks. She is happy, gay, smiling, laughing, fetching, flirtatious, animated, in short, another self.

She throws confetti in Fausto's face and giggles, her eyes shining.

He notices that she is beautiful, enchanting, and he desires her. She is an image he had seen every day. Today the image was different.

The next day Fausto tries to kiss her amidst boxes at the back of the shop. But now she has returned from the beyond, from the other side, from the fête, from spectacle to the everyday. The boxes topple. She refuses Fausto. No smiles, no sparks. The day after, Fausto is fired by her husband.

Fausto seeks revenge, as if he had been wronged.

The revenge is childish. With the help of Moraldo, he breaks into the shop at night and steals the statue of the angel.

As the lunatic saw an angel in the statue, Fausto saw his desire in the wife of his employer. It was a projection.

Had Fausto made the connection of wife and angel without knowing it? Not having the one, the wife, did he then steal the other, the angel, in recompense? He told Moraldo that the theft was to right a wrong, to settle a debt.

Reality is there if only you can see it.

On the other hand, on New Year's Eve, the wife was different. I saw it too.

SEE ALSO: CLOWNS 1, CLOWNS 2

Anita

Anita Ekberg acted in four Fellini films.

She had a major role in two of these: *La dolce vita* and *Le tentazioni del Dottor Antonio*. She made a brief appearance in *I clowns* and *Intervista*. In the first two films, she played a fictional character much like herself in reality, or as others might see her in reality. In the other two films, she played herself, Anita Ekberg, 'Anita', Fellini's 'Anitona'.

To play oneself is to play with the images of oneself.

Reality and self can sometimes be hard to come by.

La dolce vita:
Sylvia in the
Fontana di Trevi

one

In *La dolce vita*, Anita is the movie star Sylvia with whom Marcello falls in love, rather, he worships her. Anita, as Sylvia, plays Anita as Ekberg. All of these personae are the movie star whose body is spectacle and an object deified. Anita-Sylvia-Ekberg are versions of the same. The versions are disproportionate to those of a 'normal' woman because of Anita's divine beauty, because of her scale and dimensions, and because of her multiplicity, founded on the possibilities she offers others to project their desires upon her, to make her their own.

Anita is literally larger than life, a goddess.

When Fellini first met Anita Ekberg at her hotel in Rome, he said he felt like a schoolboy. He was in awe of her magnificence. For him, she was an unattainable, magical creature from another universe, from fairyland.

Fellini said he was transported, in raptures … and very hesitant.

This 'real' scene of an Anita created by Fellini's desires resembles the scene of Marcello with Anita just before dawn at the Fontana di Trevi in *La dolce vita* where she is in the basin of the fountain, drenched, standing beside the statues, as mythical in her being as the statues.

These scenes are like the visit of Rubini to the movie star's dressing room at Cinecittà in *Intervista*. Rubini is nervous, wide-eyed, with a noticeable pimple on his nose (penis), as declarative as an erection.

When Fellini heard Anita speak he felt he could relax(!).

She had the voice of a small girl. It was ludicrous as are all realisations.

Anita in Fellini's films is without personality, character or identity. She is an image, a projected presence, a dream. It is not she who is there but our wishes in her guise, our perspective which she embodies.

two

In *Le tentazioni del Dottor Antonio*, the character played by Anita Ekberg has no name, nor, strictly speaking, an existence.

She is an immense cartoon, a gigantic image in a black low-cut dress lying

across the length of a huge billboard on an empty lot within a poster advertising milk. Her breasts and body are ample, sexy and maternal at once.
Her lips are like the lips of a vagina. Her teeth are strong, shiny, milky white.

Dottor Antonio is repelled by the image (because he is puritanical) and
attracted by it (because he is puritanical). It evokes his imagination and
troubles his conscience. The ambiguity brings the image to life on the
screen as alluring and terrible. It is an Anita animated, emerging from the
billboard in the flesh of her unreal voluptuous proportions. She is cartoon
made flesh and flesh as comic cartoon. In the flesh, on-screen, she is only
another image, like the one on the billboard, parodied in mirrors of
reflected immensities.

She has no location outside her images.

Anita is monstrous and beautiful, a King Kong of beauty. She calls to Dottor Antonio, like a siren, picks him up like King Kong might a young girl,
places him tenderly between her breasts. Her breasts become for him a
children's slide and Dottor Antonio glides on them, is enveloped by them.
He is made a child by his longings and, relative to Anita and her breasts,
assumes the dimensions of a child.

She is a giant, an immense mother, and he a Lilliputian, a tiny, fright-
ened, needy infant.

Sylvia, in *La dolce vita*, is off-screen, off the set, a movie star in the flesh.
She is also the image of an image, the replica of the movie star Anita
Ekberg. Ekberg, image and flesh, is, though at a different level to Sylvia,
the image of herself. Anita, in *Le tentazioni*, is the metamorphosis of one
image into another just like it.

Four images of multiple incarnations are in play: on the billboard, on the
screen, in the mind of Antonio, as Anita Ekberg.

And perhaps a fifth, our projection.

Fellinian images are at a border between desire and reality, the subjective
and the objective. They seem to be reflected, the image of an image, or
more precisely projected, as if they are what we wish them to be while the

distance between the wish and a view that Fellini imposes of their 'reality'
is the source of their mystery, their grotesqueness, their self-parody. It creates a fascination because no image, no sight is ever stable.

The women that Fellini endows with attributes associated with sexual
attractiveness are luscious giants, not his meagre sweet angels: Gelsomina,
Cabiria, Paola.

The sisters of Anita are Saraghina (*Otto e mezzo*), the whores of Rome
(*Roma*), Volpina, Gradisca and the tobacconist in *Amarcord*, the giantess
and her two dwarfs in *Casanova*, and the oversize women in *Intervista*
bathed and oiled by oily men.

Such women transform their admirers into children and it is men as children who have created these women and imagined them as mother and
whore. The men are ludicrous baby Oedipi not concerned with a father to
murder but enthralled at a mother to fuck.

Many of the women are mature in age as they are in proportion, *tardone*,
late and ripe.

Some, like Saraghina, Volpina, the giantess in *Casanova*, and Antonio's
Anita are terrifying or/and physically revolting. It is not so much the terror
of being overpowered and dominated as the fear of being enveloped, literally absorbed, a return to the womb, both inviting and repellent.

These women are essentially maternal.

Antonio's projection of the woman on the billboard (and similar projections by Marcello, Guido, Titta, Snàporaz) is incestuous.

The incest is not the incest of intercourse but the pleasure of regression,
to the darkness and fluidity of the womb, to being lost, afloat in the soft
fullness of a body, in the suckling of heavy breasts.

The slide made of Anita's breasts by Dottor Antonio is uterine. He is
sliding back into his infancy and beyond.

The regression touches death.

three
Fellini's films have the quality of phantasies linked to the prenatal.

His films are often set underground or on an above ground which seems underground as in *Roma* (the popular street scenes) and *Fellini-Satyricon* (the street of whores). There are scenes under tents, tables, platforms, skirts, in caves, oratorios, sewers, steam baths, Turkish baths, corridors, catacombs, hulls of ships, tunnels, excavations, slides, tubes, shelters, train compartments, labyrinths, theatres, stages, at the back of trucks, at the circus, in huts, cemeteries, on sets, in the cinema.

In *Agenzia matrimoniale*, the reporter is led through a maze of corridors by giggling children until he arrives at the marriage bureau. The journey is like that of Gelsomina at the wedding celebration when she is led by the children through doors and halls and rooms to the room of the laughing idiot child, the *lunatico*, and it is like the labyrinth in *Fellini-Satyricon*, and the alleyways of Venice and the secret passages of palazzi for Casanova on his way to a sexual engagement in *Casanova*. Casanova's last engagement is with a mechanical lifesize doll with whom he dances a dance of impotence and of death.

The city of women is an enclosed underground city, an immense Luna Park of the uterus resembling Fellini's whore houses in *Roma*. They induce dizziness, anxiety, thrills, a *jouissance* … but as made for children, like a roller coaster, or the rolling deck of the ocean liner *Gloria N* in *E la nave va*.

In almost all Fellini's films after *La dolce vita*, exteriors are exteriors constructed in an interior on the set. They pullulate, amass, overheat, overwhelm, liquefy, are tubular, undulate, and can be fun like Snàporaz's slide down the tubes in *La città delle donne*, the slide to pleasure for Giulietta in *Giulietta degli spiriti*.

four

In *I clowns*, as Fellini is engaged in making his documentary on clowns, he comes across Anita at a circus camping ground where she is surveying tigers in cages. She is hoping to buy a tiger, she says. She makes her hands into claws, scratches the air, scrunches up her face and roars like a tiger.

'Volpina' is a wolf cub bitch. The name 'Saraghina' comes from 'sarago', a Mediterranean fish, striated and darkly coloured, whose flesh is prized.

Both women inhabit the beach. The sarago is a relative of the monster fish hauled up on the beach at the end of *La dolce vita*.

One of Guido's fantasies in *Otto e mezzo* is to have a harem.

In the harem scene in the film, he controls his women autocratically with a whip, treating them as you would tigers or lions or other wild animals in a circus.

In *Amarcord*, there is an oriental harem scene and a harem master behaving like an animal trainer.

The scenes of whores in *Roma*, *Fellini-Satyricon* and *Casanova* and of women in *La città delle donne* are like the harem scenes and animal scenes. Women are compared to exotic circus beasts, like Anita.

The entrances of the circus big top curl like the lips of the vagina.

Inside the tent is the circus arena, like an imaginary womb of creatures, lights, noise, colour, smells, warmth, gurglings and chaos. Fellini spoke of the movie theatre as a uterus in foetal darkness, filled with apparitions. The cinema for him is ritualistic, mythic, sacred, ancient and deeply maternal.

Anita, for Fellini, is the essence of film.

Fellini made the womb twice over in his films.

The film theatre for Fellini was like a womb and to watch a film was to relive the prenatal experience of the womb. Deleuze likened Fellini's films to biological organisms: amoebic, permeable, fluid, fantastic, bubbling.

The womb of the cinema, writ large, was Woman embodied by Anita, Anitona.

five

When Fellini's characters leave the provinces to come to Rome, it appears that they leave a real world for a fabulous one. Rome is spectacle, the circus, cinema, fantasy, liberation, dream, parade, colour, noise, music, fanfare.

When Fellini first came to Rome in 1938, he arrived with his mother.

His mother soon left to return to Rimini. For the mother who left, Fellini found another to devote himself to, the mother Rome to whom he had come. Rome (and the cinema) was a mother without the constraints of a mother, without her repressiveness and the repressiveness of the provinces: family, marriage, responsibility, conformity.

Rome was mythically founded by Romulus and Remus who were suckled by a she-wolf.

At the opening of *I clowns*, the little boy, Fellini, narrated in the voice of the adult Fellini, watches from his window in the middle of the night as the tent of the Big Top goes up. It is his entry into a dream world.

His mother warns him about the circus, about being carried off by gypsies, or worse. He goes nevertheless … or, he goes therefore.

Fellini tells the story of running away from home to join the circus.

This story of running away did not occur, yet it is a true story.

Fellini went to Rome and never returned to Rimini to live. He remained permanently in the make-believe world of his construction so passionate was his belief in the truth of dreams and his attachment to that truth. The dreams, maternal and sensual, took the place of the maternal real. It was a happier place than the real. It was a liberation from it.

six

She (Anita) is not a woman, she's a goddess.

Anita and Juno, the fecund ancestral 'Great Mother' …

Ivo Salvini, in *La voce della luna*, calms the agitated spectators who witness the striptease of the no longer young woman (a *tardona*) by relating to them the story of Juno who created the Milky Way from the milk in her breasts.

I wonder if the visions of chaos so present in Fellini's films and the association of the anarchic Augusto Clown with that chaos is not also the indifference of the womb. And I wonder if the orderliness of the symbolic associated with the White Clown and maturity is what you emerge into, are born into from the womb. These two worlds are necessary to each other. Each is the other that they require. Their conjunction is what Fellini requires and his films require to be whole and complete.

Energy, creativity, fantasy, for Fellini, comes from the fluidity of the womb, a place where you can be imaginatively and where the sources of imagination are.

The sacred is in odd locations.

SEE ALSO: FELLINI, RIMINI, RUBINI, (THE) SHERIFF, ZOOLOGY

(The) Beyond

In Jean Cocteau's film *Orphée*, made in 1950, the main characters, Eurydice and Orphée, descend to the other world, that of the dead who are still living. A decade later Cocteau made his last film *Le Testament d'Orphée* where Cocteau, the poet, is a character in the film who takes passage to the other world to meet the characters from *Orphée* who condemn him (to live) for having created them and left them in limbo.

Jean-Luc Godard's *Alphaville* is inspired, I think, by both Cocteau films. More generally, Godard's films of the 1960s, then again of the 1980s, create characters who belong to a world of film, a world alive only in images. The characters in the world of the present in the Godard film we see are citations of characters from other films, that is characters from other worlds which have passed. The characters in the film who are citations from other films will in turn become citations passing from a present of enunciation to a past of their enunciated.

Citation is a resurrection and also a passing to a beyond.

The characters who cite other characters in Godard's films are like

Il bidone: peasants with faggots like angels

Rouch's Africans in Treichville in *Moi, un noir*, who play at being Dorothy Lamour, Eddie Constantine and Edward G. Robinson. These stars of the cinema become mythical, legendary beings in Treichville. Entering a fictional identity is a way to find yourself.

Edward G. Robinson and Dorothy Lamour for the Africans are the Orphée and Eurydice of Cocteau. Pasolini made an African Oresteia.

Godard's *Histoire(s) du cinéma* is a journey of the film-maker, Godard (like Cocteau), into the world of film from which he brings back fragments of other films into his own film, his *Histoire(s)* of *histoires*, images dislocated from the narratives they once inhabited which now float free. Godard's film is literally a resurrection of the cinema, and an encyclopaedic one. It is a history where there is no duration, or chronology, or past or present.

As with the Cocteau films, images and figures are torn from their context, from the world they had lived in, from the fictions which created them and provoked their and our desires. As traces and citations in Godard's *Histoire(s)* they live again, but it is another existence, elsewhere than where they had been.

These journeys to the beyond call to mind Dante especially in *Histoire(s)* and in Cocteau's *Le Testament*, the poet entering the nether world of images and their associations, guided, accompanied as Dante was by a Virgil, another poet. One other film perhaps should be added, Fritz Lang's *The Testament of Dr Mabuse*. Not only does Mabuse enter another world, speeds towards it, but as with the underworld to which poets descend in the Cocteau and the Godard, all things are subject to metamorphoses in *Mabuse* including the identity of Mabuse himself. And the journeys call up as well Joyce's *Ulysses* somewhere between Dante and Cocteau and Godard, displacements of the underworld motif in epic poetry

Pier Paolo Pasolini also made these journeys into the past of images to restore to them their power to metamorphose, recombine, reassert themselves thus confounding and enriching time and identity.

Medea, Teorema, Porcile, Edipo Re are explicit returns to legendary worlds

as is Pasolini's *Salò*. The films are shadowed by spectres from the past, past images and thereby shadowed by death. Pasolini, like Cocteau, in his use of classical references and his classicising of the vulgar, creates a sense that what you see is a world of shadows neither living nor dead. The world that has passed and yet is re-evoked is made to live again in a new configuration, to live differently as fragments.

The fragment, the citation are free.

The beyond where Eurydice was taken and where Orphée pursued her is a kingdom of images without time, a place of life and death, present and past, reality and legend. These qualities, their boundlessness and instability, are the essence of cinema.

Fellini's *Il viaggio di G. Mastorna*, a film scripted but not made, reverberates like these other films with this essence of images caught in a nether world of timelessness. It is evident in Fellini's funereal recreations of the classical and the historical in *Il Casanova di Federico Fellini*, *Fellini-Satyricon*, *Roma*, *Amarcord*, in the voyage of the dead in *E la nave va* to scatter

La dolce vita: Christ transported over Rome

the ashes of Edmea Tetua on a plastic sea, and in the farewells of *Intervista* and *Ginger e Fred* filled with decay, death and passing, mocked by disintegration.

These are among his most beautiful and cruel films.

The presence of memory and of dream locations, of being in a beyond outside of time are characteristic of his films after *La dolce vita*.

It is already hinted at in the earlier films.

Fellini's Anita Ekberg in *La dolce vita* is a goddess of the cinema and a myth of Woman, nostalgia and memory revivified, a divine creature from the beyond and from the depths.

The full force of her resurrection and its horror and joy is in *Intervista*, when Anita, blousy and old, stands beside her image as young and gorgeous from *La dolce vita*, an impossible citation across a terrible gap of time and desire.

Fellini: 'We are constructed in memory; we are simultaneously childhood, adolescence, old age and maturity.'

SEE ALSO: ANITA, MASTORNA, SPIRITS

Chaplin

In 1987, Dario Zanelli asked Fellini to choose 42 films (!) he would like to see in a summer festival of films. Fellini chose four Chaplin films in the following order: *The Kid* (1), *The Circus* (3), *City Lights* (6) and *Monsieur Verdoux* (20).

Fellini frequently mentioned Chaplin. Chaplin for him was exaggeration, excess, marginality, the tramp, in short, a clown. Chaplin belonged thereby for Fellini to music hall, variety theatre, the circus and forms of popular spectacle that Fellini loved. These had been part of his childhood along with Pinocchio, *Corriere dei piccoli*, American comics, Laurel and Hardy and Charles Dickens.

Gelsomina and Cabiria are Chaplinesque clowns. *La strada* and *Le notti di Cabiria* have clear echoes of Chaplin.

'Charlie' is a vagabond, utterly castaway, pathetic and absurd.

His costume and person point in opposed directions. All he wears is not his, hand-me-downs, patched rags. The rags, however, evoke elegance and wealth, indeed aspire to it: the bowler hat, the morning coat, the cane, the gloves, Charlie's exaggerated snobbisms, the way he pulls off his gloves,

Le notti di Cabiria: the Chaplinesque clown-like Cabiria

lights a cigarette, holds a cup. He is elegance and its caricature, nobility and its dispossession.

It is as if Charlie is a metaphysical absence as he is a social non-entity. His ambition is to be what he is not. In being what he is, he denies himself. He is his own negation, nothing at all, since the something he wishes for, to be a person, not a clown, is just outside his grasp. The history he assumes in his costume does not belong to him. The non-belonging, the non-person is himself.

Charlie has no past, no biography, no story, no future.

This is the fate of clowns. Clowns are only types, the burlesque of persons. It is the source of their comedy and their terror.

If Charlie is a clown, Chaplin is not. He movingly proved that by removing the mask of Charlie in *Limelight* and in *Monsieur Verdoux*. In *Verdoux*, Chaplin assumed all that Charlie was not. He became a person, with a history, truly elegant, not vagabond nor clown. Rather than rescuing women, he delightfully murdered them. But in his earlier best films, some chosen by Fellini for a summer festival, to which perhaps ought to be added *Modern Times*, Chaplin is never completely effaced by Charlie.

In fact, it is the relation between the two, between person and clown, reality and mask, inventor and invented, that is the appeal of Chaplin's films.

If, within the films, Charlie can be pure joy, improvisation, wit, opportunism, invention and resilience, qualities that transform the slightest object into a prop, thereby transforming the world and animating it as surely as Picasso sculpted the head of a baboon with a toy car, qualities of pastiche, citation, collage and verve at the heart of the modern, Chaplin himself has these qualities in his invention of the pastiche Charlie.

Charlie who improvises is the inspired improvisation of Chaplin.

Chaplin's history is a history of dispossession, eviction from self, an orphan deprived of what is most precious to us, childhood. Fellini begins childhood with Chaplin, begins it in joy, laughter, security, as a little person that will be. Chaplin, the non-person, becomes a clown, a burlesque of person. Fellini invents clowns, Gelsomina and Cabiria, but is never one, and perhaps for that reason these characters are confined to caricature. Charlie the clown is ever in search of Chaplin the person and Chaplin the person has no other recourse in order to be a person than to assume the mask of Charlie the clown.

The oscillation between being and non-being is the substance of Charlie Chaplin, condemned in his films to return to non-being but with the choreographed jauntiness of a flat footed dance as if embracing it.

Chaplin in the guise of Charlie was only possible in film where being and appearance are confounded, unlike theatre or circus where there are no persons, only actors and imaginary characters. The cinema, to the contrary, touches the real and that is the quality of Charlie that moves us.

Charlie the non-person is a reality.

The world that initially rejected Chaplin can only suffer and accept him as the non-person of its creation. And it is perhaps the singular and lonely terms on which Chaplin had to accept himself. For him there was no going back to the world that rejected him except to be accepted as a reject, and then as a sweet revenge to be rejected again as the murderer, but not social outcast, M. Verdoux.

At the end of *Le notti di Cabiria*, Cabiria looks at the camera momentarily, smiles, then rejoins the young players inside the film, once again becoming a character in a make believe. Is this passing complicity with the audience not also part of make believe? Is Cabiria at that moment, not Cabiria, but Giulietta? But if she is Giulietta, is Giulietta that different from Cabiria or Gelsomina or Amelia Bonetti/Ginger? What is the line, if there is one, between the character and the person?

This scene is a scene repeated by Chaplin at the end of his films, movingly in *Modern Times*, just before Charlie and the Gamin, played by Paulette Goddard, the two of them again reduced to vagabondage, hand in hand, walk into the heaven, not of an ideal world, that of normality that they had unsuccessfully sought, but into a truly ideal world of vagabondage from which there was no exit. This world marginalised by the actual world is also real but at a different, more sublime level. It is there that fantasy and invention lie, the world of the cinema where dreams come true.

Fellini multiplies masks. If there is a hint that Gelsomina, the projected caricature and distortion of the person Giulietta, has as her secret ambition to become Giulietta, to become real, to be normal, not a clown, Fellini reveals that Giulietta herself is but another mask, a version of a clown, and that caricature is a condition of existence in Fellini's worlds. Fellini plunges his clowns and his audience into a vertigo of identities that slide into instabilities where identity is uncertain because plural and false.

Fellini can take pleasure in a mechanism perfected by Chaplin, but for Chaplin the game was one of pathos tinged with melodrama, not the usual tone for Fellini. After all, Chaplin had formed 'Famous Players' with Griffith and Fairbanks. Only *La strada* perhaps has this quality, and the last moments of *Il bidone*, and the final scene of *I clowns* where the clowns dance into eternity like Charlie and the Gamin do in *Modern Times*.

In an interview with Dominique Delouche in *Cahiers du cinéma* in 1956, Fellini was asked who he would consider to be his masters in the cinema.

'Chaplin and Rossellini' he replied.

SEE ALSO: CLOWNS 1, CLOWNS 2, GIULIETTA, ROSSELLINI 1, ROSSELLINI 2

Citations 1

Georges Sadoul referring to *Giulietta degli spiriti*:

> I could, as others have done, recall Bosch, Breughel, Fini, Trouille (but not Dalì); these correspondences are not entirely arbitrary. Fellini referred to all manner of work from different cultural periods: the 'Modern Style', the *Seven Samurai* of Kurosawa, *Lola Montes* of Marcel Ophüls, (postage stamps) of the Viennese 'Secession', 1910 postcards and the 1895 films of Louis Lumière, revues in the style of Ziegfield or the Folies-Bergères with their leggy and full breasted girls, 'musicals', German Expressionism and French Impressionism, James Bond and James Joyce, Minnelli and *My Fair Lady*, Mandrake the Magician and Marcel Proust ... But let us stop here. To list all the references in this Giullietesque pandemonium would take up an entire newspaper.

And Alberto Moravia:

> ... he has used colour with very great intelligence, refinement, originality. His knowledge of various currents in modern painting is evident, for example, that of Surrealism: framings and colours that recall Magritte and groupings that recall Max Ernst.

Citations 2

Viktor Shklovsky, the Russian Formalist critic, was in love with Elsa Triolet who later became the wife of Louis Aragon. Elsa was in love with the Futurist poet, Vladimir Mayakovsky. She was the sister of Lily Brik, the wife of the Formalist critic, Osip Brik. Mayakovsky was in love with Lily. Mayakovsky, Lily Brik and Osip Brik lived together.

Shklovsky, not a Bolshevik, but a Socialist Revolutionary, was living in exile in Berlin in the 1920s after the Bolsheviks had taken power. He wrote Elsa letters of love. Elsa told him that she would not accept letters of love. She was not in love with him. She was in love with Mayakovsky. Mayakovsky, however, was not in love with her, but with her sister …

Shklovsky consented to Elsa's wishes. He did so, it may be presumed, because he was in love with her and so wrote to her letters that she would accept: passionate letters not about love.

Ginger e Fred: Pippo and Amelia as Astaire and Rogers laughing at other doubles

The letters in fact were not about love, but about being in exile from love and from the Soviet Union.

The letters were published in a book entitled *Zoo, or Letters not about Love*.

Shklovsky's book was modelled on the letters of the twelfth-century lovers, Abelard and Héloïse. Abelard was a professor in Paris and Héloïse was his young pupil. One evening, as he lay in bed, Abelard was attacked by members of her family who castrated him.

The correspondence of the lovers is in Latin in forms dictated by scholastic philosophy which Héloïse had been taught by Abelard. In the correspondence, Abelard denied their love while Héloïse adamantly insisted on it and argued for it, as that which had existed and still existed and might continue to exist.

Because she loved him and understood his pain and wished to continue their love, if only in letters, she consented to denying its past and its future as he wished for her to do as if it never was nor ever could be.

They wrote love letters to each other then not about love, he from his monastery, she from her convent.

Perhaps the love of Viktor for Elsa never existed and Shklovsky invented it in order to conform to desires and a vocation for fabulation, the mirroring of false passions, and he did so not because he loved Elsa but because he was a writer and he loved writing. As a writer Shklovsky could lose himself in writing which is an exile and an escape and a way of being close to oneself. The mask of the literary was not a way to remember but a way to forget. Abelard and Héloïse were resurrected by Shklovsky, made to live again as citations.

In the mid-1970s, Shklovsky passed through London. I was the editor of *Screen* then. The editorial board of the journal organised an interview with him. He spoke in Russian. One of our editors, Diana Matias, translated. Shklovsky set one condition for the interview: that we did not talk to him about his past. He wanted to talk of his ideas now and about the book he had just written on Eisenstein. The interview lasted for a few hours. It was sheer delight. Shklovsky was happy, youthful, funny and gay.

When I came to the office the next day, Diana said that the tape was blank.

SEE ALSO: EFFACEMENT

Clowns 1

Didn't Saint Francis call himself God's Jester?

And Lao Tse used to say: 'As soon as you conceive a thought, laugh at it.'

The cinema has always been the same thing: a rickety camera with someone behind it filming a clown moving in front of it.

In Rossellini's *Francesco, giullare di Dio*, on which Fellini worked, as Saint Francis prays and praises God, the creator, the birds sing with him. In Pasolini's *Uccellacci e uccellini* (*Hawks and Sparrows*), the clown pair, Totò and Ninetto, are doubled as Innocenti Totò and Innocenti Ninetto in the present and as friar Ciccillo and friar Ninetto in a medieval past. In the present the pair talk to a Marxist crow, whom they eat (eating the father). In the medieval past, Cicillio learns the language of the birds and talks to them. Friar Ninetto dances his whirling, skipping dances of joy.

I clowns: Clowns acting like clowns in a make-believe circus

Friar Ciccillo is Rossellini's San Francesco revivified.

Rossellini's *India* has elephants, tigers and monkeys. The animal world is a mirror world of the human world, mocking it and fulfilling it.

The following is an exchange between Peisetairos and Iris in Aristophanes' *The Birds*:

PEISETAIROS: … state your business here.

IRIS: My business? Why, I am bearing the following message from my father Zeus
   to mankind:
   Let holocausts make glad thy gods
   And mutton barbecues on beefy altars toast,
   Yea, till every street doth reek with roast
   ambrosially.

PEISETAIROS: Hmm. I think he wants a sacrifice. But to which gods?

IRIS: To *which* gods? To *us*, of course. Who else could he mean?

PEISETAIROS: But that's quite absurd. *You*, gods? I mean, really!

IRIS: Name me any other gods.

PEISETAIROS: Why, the Birds, madam …

Kenneth McLeish, in a study of Aristophanes, noted that Peisetairos and Euelpides are a double clown act of straight man and fool. He compares them to the couples Laurel and Hardy and Groucho Marx and Margaret Dumont. The double clown act of Peisetairos and Euelpides in *The Birds* is also evident in Aristophanes' *The Frogs* and *The Wasps*. The human/animal comparisons are central to his clowns and caricatures.

Laurel and Hardy graced Fellini's childhood, a doubled classicism.

SEE ALSO: ZOOLOGY

Clowns 2

Bario in *I clowns* is a White Clown, an Italian, with a carrot-coloured mop for hair and a face chalked white.

At the end of *I clowns* there is a mock funeral for the Augusto Clown, Fischietto. The funeral degenerates into a frantic, frenetic pandemonium caused by the clowns not unlike the close of *Prova d'orchestra* when the players riot and the oratorio is destroyed, and of *Otto e mezzo*, just before Guido finds his way out of chaos. Bario, who has taken part in the funeral spectacle, is out of breath. He steps out of the circus ring to rest.

Bario is old. He belongs to a circus of the past, the circus that the funeral reenacts and also lays to rest. The funeral of the clown is at the same time a funeral for the circus and for the memories of it and of the childhood shaped by it.

When the funeral performance is over, Fellini, who is interior to the film playing himself, a film director making a documentary on clowns and the

I clowns: real clowns in a false performance of being clowns

passing of the circus in the film *I clowns*, announces that the film(s) have come to an end, both the documentary film and the film which contains it. Fellini orders the technicians to extinguish the lights.

As these spectacles end another begins.

Bario and Fellini are now alone on the empty set of the circus documentary and the set of the film which filmed it. Bario narrates to 'signor Fellini' the story of Frou Frou, an Augusto Clown who had been his clown partner in the past. In *I clowns*, Bario reenacts that past but is no longer outside of the reenactment. This film of remembrance and the funeral are both performed for 'signor Fellini' …

As Bario relates his story, Fellini presents it in images. He brings Bario's memory and narration to 'life', into the fiction and the imaginary of film.

One day, Bario says, the director of the circus told him that Frou Frou had died.

Bario was distraught. He looked everywhere for Frou Frou, unbelieving, uncomprehending.

Was it possible that Frou Frou was dead?

He called out for him: 'Frou Frou', 'Frou Frou'.

There was no reply.

He picked up his trumpet and sounded it in the empty circus ring, a lament, a circus blues.

Suddenly, from high up in the circus stands, another trumpet responded to his.

It was played by Frou Frou.

Frou Frou continued the melody of Bario's lament. Each trumpet played a fragment. Together they established a harmony from the past and of the past.

Bario's trumpet had brought Frou Frou back into existence as Fellini had called into existence what Bario remembered thus calling up Frou Frou into the shadowy existence of images. There were two couples now: Bario and Frou Frou, and Bario and Fellini.

Like Orpheus, like Cocteau, like Welles, Fellini often descended into
another world peopled with his and others' dreams and memories.

Bario was in his splendid costume.

Frou Frou was in his ordinary one, a suit and a small bowler hat.

The two clowns played their melancholy song of sadness, joy and chagrin, a happiness of longed-for desire made present and so palpable as to
seem real.

The joy was also a sadness. The reality evoked was only the phantasm of
memory, more real than real, but unpossessable. Just so the film, *I clowns*,
and the funeral within it recalling a memory, bringing it to life in images
including the memory of death which it mocks in the absurd clown funeral,
a clown's affirmation against death, which is the remembering and the parody of what is remembered by way of a desperate pandemonium.

The trumpet lament is like the one that accompanies Gelsomina in *La
strada* and which touches Zampanò's soul after he discovers Gelsomina is
dead.

Bario and Frou Frou descend the steps calling to each other with their
trumpets.

So long as there is music, there is Frou Frou.

The two clowns meet in the centre of the ring.

Before they exit, the music ends.

At that moment they are wiped from the screen and the image itself is
effaced into darkness.

The film emerges from its unreality of an imagined life into the everyday
of life. The dream work of the film is at an end.

And then all the lights of all the films that were the texture of *I clowns*
are extinguished.

Frou Frou was never on the screen. Only his shadow had been present, an
image of an image. Clowns are not real beings. They mock reality including the reality of death.

Only an Augusto Clown, like Fischietto, could deride the terror of his own death by clowning and thereby escape it. The appearance of Frou Frou is the same escape from death into the unreality of images of desire.

The clowns of I *clowns* are the clowns of childhood.

The film greets them with joy, brings them to life and bids them farewell.

White Clowns are over-confident, well-dressed, adult, arrogant, brave, disciplined.

Augusto Clowns are anarchic, infantile, slovenly, clumsy, cowardly, idiotic.

They require each other. They are each the other's half without which neither could exist.

The Augusto Clown needs the White Clown to govern his disorderly impulses so that the dreams these express might be realised. And the White Clown requires the Augusto for there to be dreams at all.

Together the two clowns are a harmony of maturity and creativity.

Maturity is found by Zampanò in his reconciliation with Gelsomina; it is found by Guido who had been at odds with himself in *Otto e mezzo*; and it is found by Snàporaz when he wakes from his dream of the city of women that had been the embodiment of his fears and desires and infantilism.

The reconciliation of the clowns and of their contrasting attributes is a matter of images, already indicated as unreal. Images are offered as a play and their structure and order as the regulation of play. Both aspects are in the image and are its principal constituents: desire that gives birth to the image and consciousness that gives it form.

These are the essential elements of the trumpet duet between Frou Frou and Bario which brings together the two qualities. The image is fantastic and symbolic, divided and harmonious, the wonder of the child and the power of the adult.

Film is like a circus for Fellini and the clown its crucial element. Clowning is the structural heart of the Fellinian image.

Fellinian images are haunted by decay, death, disappearance and disillusion, inescapable realities which his films and its clowns seek to overcome, but which call them back to order, as in a coming back to reality.

This presence of reality and hence of death as a constraint and a limit is not, as it is in melodrama, social or tragic, but a condition of life as is the will to transcend it.

Fellini deals in eternities.

The film image is double-sided, the trace of what is no longer and what may never have been, and a testament to the capacity of the image to transform reality into what can be dreamt, a possible reality, the transfiguration of the world thereby and its redemption.

Film is a descent and leap into another world, across a barrier into what can be imagined and dreamt and remembered.

I clowns is a memorial to a childhood of clowns and the enchantment of clowns including the terror of them.

The film is their requiem and their return to life.

It is thereby a reconciliation.

SEE ALSO: CONMEN (*BIDONISTI*), ROSSELLINI, SPIRITS, TRUMPETS

Conmen (*bidonisti*)

In melodrama hopes are raised, desires provoked, then disappointed. The intensity of disappointment is in direct relation to the intensity of desire. The gap between the two is at the heart of melodrama. The negation of desire by the force of reality is sad and painful to watch and usually tragic and destructive for those involved, as in the films of Visconti, for example.

The trick, the swindle, the *bidonata*, also plays on desire but by an elaborate game of masquerade and seduction, the confidence trick, a low-life parody of middle-class tragedy.

The trickster works in disguise. He is Oscar in *Le notti di Cabiria*, who feigns love to the whore Cabiria who wants love so desperately that she believes Oscar who then takes her money.

In melodrama, things do not work out because reality is too powerful. Visconti has no need of a trickster. In the *bidone*, things are not supposed to work out. The trick is too tempting not to perform it.

Melodrama frightens and horrifies. The *bidone* is an entertainment, a clowning about.

Il bidone: Augusto as a bishop swindles a peasant

For Fellini, the trickster is essential in his films and the operator of them. Fellini is his films' principal trickster.

The tragic consequences of melodrama are tragic because unintended. The *bidone* is pure intention.

The *bidone* is an open manipulation of desire. The manipulation is present from the beginning, the motive for what happens and the cause of events. The success of the *bidone* is less in the winning of a stake than in the pleasure of the play. It is a way of life. The *bidonisti* may have the advantage of money or sex, but it is the game that most counts for them. The victims are victims of their own desires, complicit in their victimisation (seduction), more than willing indeed, like Cabiria.

A *bidonata* is the grotesque of melodrama, the parody of it, melodrama deformed. It exaggerates it merrily.

Melodrama is essentially social and political. Desires are provoked by the social repressions and institutions that deny them, hence the social criticism and the explosiveness of the form, an individual crushed by society, society exposed or torn by passions unleashed in the individual.

The *bidonata* is a consequence of human nature: to take advantage of others and often for the fun of it as its principal gain, like a prank, the practical joke. Money is involved but it is not the goal. It is more a means to the entertainment.

High drama and intense emotion do not belong to the world of tricksters and masquerade. The *bidonata* belongs to a tradition of *carnevale*, of circus, clowning, slapstick, irreverence.

The melodramatic tradition is purely *bourgeois* whereas the *bidonata* is more popular and less refined. For Fellini to have chosen it as a central form and activity makes it part of his renewal of forms by the resurrection of old forms characteristic of modernism.

Bidonisti can be criminals, as is the criminal band in *Il bidone*. But for Fellini, they are essentially seducers, mischief-makers, naughty children, disrupters, clowns, pure performers, acting silly for the fun of it.

They reenact an eternal and ancient drama and not, as in melodrama, a socially and historically defined one.

The subject of most Fellini films is the *bidonata*. His main protagonists are *bidonisti* with few exceptions.

Bidonisti belong with the angels, clowns and monsters who inhabit Fellini's world. The awful things they do are outrageous, but like the acts of badly behaved children, they are directed at the adult world, against maturity, responsibility, orderliness, conformity. Their acts are often silly, sometimes terrifying, but it is play. They don't mean to do harm though often they do. Mischief may have consequences but fundamentally it lacks any other intention than the delight of mischief itself.

Jacques Tati is a variant of the clown but not of the prankster because Tati, not unlike Buster Keaton in *The General*, wants to do good. The resultant havoc is unintentional. He is so careful to be good that his gestures become extreme, out of kilter and askew, to set up a chain reaction of disasters. The more good he seeks, the more trouble and destruction he causes.

Bidonisti dress up, make believe, fool people, seduce, cavort, flirt, and never tell the truth. Casanova is a *bidonista*. Pippo–Fred is a *bidonista*. Fellini's seducers are *bidonisti*: Fausto, Fernando Rivoli, Marcello, Snàporaz. Eventually age catches up with them, playing the final trick, like what

Il bidone: Augusto dying

becomes of Pippo–Fred and all the old clowns in *I clowns*. No one believes them any more and the trick doesn't work, a sign of tiredness and despair, a coming to consciousness, like the death of Augusto in *Il bidone* as a result of an unconvincing *bidonata*.

Reality has the last word in death.

It is the ultimate *bidone*.

Seductions are swindles.

Even when the trickster is criminal there is something unserious, endearing about the *bidone* committed. For example, Fernando Rivoli, dressed as a comic book sheik in *Lo sceicco bianco*, seeking to seduce Wanda, in love with him in his masquerade as a fairy tale oriental prince that she and thousands like her dream of in the provinces and who are sketched in the comic books they read.

Rivoli's unreality and the fantasy of Wanda's desires are his advantage. He becomes in every respect her (provincial) dream come true. Rivoli is a dream that is produced by a pathetic ordinariness.

Her seduction by him needs little encouragement. Rivoli has simply to exist. She has seduced herself.

Wanda lives in the make-believe of *fotoromanzi*. She writes letters to her sheik calling herself 'Bambola appassionata'.

The *bidonisti* can do harm without really meaning to. They are immature, irresponsible, lack morality, but are not thereby immoral though they do immoral things. They lack evil intention, or a sense of guilt, grown-upness.

Their pranks are a matter of their nature.

And their nature is semi-magical, marvellous.

Bidonisti perform *bidonate* and that is that.

Fellini is a *bidonista* … sort of.

His cinema is a *bidone* … sort of. He differs from his *bidonisti* because they play tricks whereas Fellini wants to show you the trick. He is a second-order *bidonisti* and there is no harm in him because there are no real consequences.

It is only a film after all.

Fellini is not an illusionist.

He displays the cardboard and the fakery. It is what you want or what he provokes you to want. He shows you everything, the consequence, how it has been done and is proud of the trick, revelling in it. In showing you that, you learn something, and not that you are dupe of your desires, but rather what your desires are.

Like the seducer, Fellini is egotistical at heart, but it is not power he wants.

Fellini is innocent and childlike in his mischief and at the same time conscious and controlled. The one side is his inspiration, the other his skill of expression.

His films clown about and Fellini, happily, clowns too, but he, without misgivings, gives the trick away. That is *his* entertainment and ours.

Fellini is a moralist who never moralises.

Il bidone opens with three men driving in a car with Vatican licence plates along a country road. There is the chauffeur, a priest, an archbishop. They stop at a farmhouse and tell the farmers a story about buried treasure on their land, buried there by a thief ages ago. The clerics have a map which details where the treasure is which they dig up as the peasants look on.

The treasure is a chest of jewellery and precious stones.

The clerics tell the farmers that the treasure is theirs on condition they pay the church a sum of money for perpetual mass for the thief whose treasure it was. The farmers, greedy and calculating, consent. They find the money and hand it over to the archbishop.

The car drives away leaving the treasure and the farmers behind.

The men in the car are *bidonisti* dressed as churchmen. The story is false, the jewellery fake. Only the desires of the peasant and the money they give for these desires are real.

The *bidonisti* have played their parts.

It could be a circus skit of clowns. It is a prank.

Yet, life itself is this prank, hence the melancholy of Fellini.

Il bidone is fundamentally, like most of Fellini's films, an accumulation of *bidonate*, of 'numbers'. Slum dwellers are swindled, a wretched guy at a petrol station is swindled, other peasants are swindled by a repeat of the buried treasure caper. The reward for the *bidonisti* is less the money, than the joy of the game, the laughter.

These are clowns and clowns are aristocrats.

Finally, Augusto tries the super swindle to betray his friends of the money he has taken from the peasants.

They are not fooled. There is no laughter. They beat him up and leave him beside the road where he dies, the death of a clown.

Perhaps, for Fellini, God is the ultimate trickster who would have us believe that He exists and that the world is meaningful. If God does exist for Fellini, and he says that He does, it is not because the world is meaningful, but because it is not. The absurdity of the world is Fellini's and our opportunity.

This is the gift of God.

Bidonisti are full of fantasy.

They invent tricks.

They may be vile and depraved, false and manipulative, but they are so as clowns, that is as an act. Their inventions are minute, passionate, ferocious with a touch of poetry.

It is difficult not to like them.

They are ancient popular figures of the circus, of Punch and Judy, of marionette shows, of the *commedia dell'arte*, of caricature, of travelling players, like Zampanò. Fellini and his cinema revivifies these, restores them to life.

Samuel Beckett, with his clowns and vaudeville vagrants, is a relative of Fellini's.

And so too is Pasolini and his puppets, the Neapolitan marionette, Totò, and the giggly Ninetto who accompanies him, as is Renoir and his Boudu and the bookseller, and Marceau, the poacher, in *La Règle du jeu*, all honest men.

SEE ALSO: CLOWNS 2, ILLUSIONISM, (THE) SHERIFF, SPECTACLE

Dance

Most Fellini films have dance sequences. Usually there are several in a single film.

In *La dolce vita*, there are ten dance numbers. In *Otto e mezzo*, there are nine. In *La città delle donne*, seven. In *La voce della luna*, five.

The dance numbers are various.

There are chorus lines, New Year's Eve balls, striptease, rock and roll, belly dancing, the Charleston, the waltz, the mambo, cha-cha-cha, jive, tap dancing, Flamenco, a clicking of heels. There is dancing at weddings, parties, celebrations, discothèques, night clubs, on stage, at rehearsals, in public toilets. There are dancing dwarfs, Serbs, clowns, peasants, whores, transvestites, orientals and gays. Children are danced with, and dolls. There is a bullfight dance. There is piggy-back dancing.

The dances are not compelling as dance.

There is no Fred Astaire, Cyd Charisse or Gene Kelly in Fellini's films, no contribution to dance, no performance to cheer. Those without talent for dance, dance nevertheless: Masina and Mastroianni in *Ginger e Fred*, the chorus girls in *Luci del varietà*, in *I vitelloni*, in *La dolce vita*, the ballroom dancing of amateurs.

Dance in Fellini is seldom a complete performance. It is a fragment only, an impulse.

In American musicals, dance is presented to the audience as a performance, as a spectacle which draws it outside the fiction which has motivated it. The motivation sustains the performance providing it with a narrative significance which the dance exceeds yet is absorbed by, dramatic action in one register, spectacle in another.

Characters dance their love as an expression of the narrative with a skill that makes the expression admirable as pure movement, rhythm, colour and energy. The emotion of characters is expressed in the formal beauty of the dance, at once meaning and form, as in Gene Kelly's title dance of joy in *Singin' in the Rain*.

Dances in a Fellini film are usually half-finished, merely glimpsed, often slovenly, laughable, mocking, absurd. They can have considerable narrative force, the dance of Casanova with a doll, for example. The performance does not exceed the character for its value as dance, but becomes an instrument of caricature, of a distance between sentiment and expression, not their realisation, but their dissolution.

Donald O'Connor in *Singin' in the Rain* makes fun of something in his dancing, performs a comic dance routine as an instance of a dazzling, magical performance of dance. In a Fellini film, the dances are comic because they open an unsustainable gap between what is and what is supposed to be, between a reality and a projection upon it. Whereas dance and narrative recombine in the American musical, in the films of Fellini they create a gulf of distance and of unease, often exploded in laughter.

In *Otto e mezzo*, the slut Saraghina dances the rumba on the beach in front of Guido and his school mates in exchange for money. She is monstrous in size and mien.

She emerges from out of a cave. Her bottom is huge, her lips fleshy, her eyes black, omnivorous, her tongue quivering, tremulous, darting, her legs thick, sagging elephant legs. Her hips and thighs shake. They stir up the agitated, excited, enthralled schoolboys.

Guido is minuscule, a Lilliputian, angelic.

The discrepancies in it are the point of the scene.

Saraghina's dance has characteristics general in Fellini films.

It is *disproportionate*: the immense Saraghina and the little boys.

It is *exaggerated*: every gesture, every aspect is excessive.

It is *antithetical*: a dance of seduction that is revolting.

It is *parodic*: it mimics, ridicules itself, is a travesty.

It is *false*: everything is staged and choreographed.

There are many other examples: the El Muchacho dance in *Luci del varietà*,

Fernando Rivoli's dance at the refreshment kiosk with Wanda in *Lo sceicco bianco*, Cabiria's dance with Lazzari in the night club in *Le notti di Cabiria*, Sylvia's dance with Frankie in *La dolce vita*, the tap dance routine at the variety show in *Roma*, Casanova's dance with the doll in *Il Casanova di Federico Fellini*, the dance of the dwarfs in *Ginger e Fred*, the dance of Marcello and Anita in *La dolce vita* represented in *Intervista* touched by decay, the striptease in *La voce della luna*.

The dances are travesties, a distorted mirror, resemblances, like metaphors, but the terms are semblances of the thing to itself, that is, a caricature, a mocking double.

The caricature in form and intention belongs to the comic book and the funny face sketch: a big nose made bigger, thick lips thickened, generous hips more generous still. Anita, already large, becomes Junoesque. In *La dolce vita*, *Otto e mezzo* and *Le tentazioni del Dottor Antonio*, Anita's disproportion is the result of a subjective distortion of perspective, the projection produced by the regard of her by a character. It is like a distorting mirror at Luna Park. It is a vision stretched beyond truth which nevertheless reveals something really there, but hidden, until it is distorted. The caricature is a means of knowing because the perspective that it creates reveals desire.

The metaphor forms likenesses of unlike things. It surprises, confounds,

Le notti di Cabiria: Cabiria dances at the pick-up place

La dolce vita:
Sylvia at the
night club

astonishes, gives birth to the new in strange juxtapositions. Modernism revelled in it, particularly the Surrealists. The distanced and disconnected were set side by side, a montage of shock, a spark, a leap to catapult the imagination and unleash an energy.

The caricature, a minor art, lacks this power. In it, likenesses are between like things. Most often it degrades but not without affection.

Exaggeration makes images of objects. Caricature does not represent. It mocks representation by disparity. By such means reality loses its resistance, consistency and objectivity, literally it is stretched out of shape, thereby surrendered to artifice and once accomplished, once transformed, is spectacle, 'number', variety, fantasy, and in its peculiar way, by this sullying and bringing down.

At worst, caricature sentimentalises and softens.

There are however rare scenes of the sublime in Fellini.

The question is not what Fellini signifies by dance, but what he does with
it.

For him, it is an instrument of artifice, to engage the imagination in order
to refashion things. He creates in each film an entirely new world doubled
as an open imposture of the ordinary one. The real, parodied by its duplicate, becomes other to itself, wearing a mask, in costume, with a red nose,
a funny face.

The distorting elements of caricature are lines, colour, space, light, bulk,
shape, the reality of all images. Though taking us toward the unreal, it takes
us at the same time, and necessarily, to these tools and instruments for
refashioning the world, those of artifice, the substances of the cinema.

In this way, dances in Fellini's films are forms.

An exchange from Pasolini's *La ricotta*:

(Above and right) *Ginger e Fred*: Pippo and Amelia play Ginger and Fred at a
television spectacular

TEGLIESERA: Fourth and final question: what is your opinion ... of our great Federico Fellini?

FILM DIRECTOR (*inspired*): He dances!

He pauses, thinks deeply, concentrates, but then not finding anything better than that ineffable phrase, repeats it.

FILM DIRECTOR: He dances!

TEGLIESERA (*bashful, ceremonious*): Aaaaaaah ... Ta, ta ... .Congratulations, goodbye ...

SEE ALSO: ANITA, CLOWNS

Documentary

Prova d'orchestra pretends to be a television documentary about an orchestra rehearsal.

The pretence is openly avowed. It is the pretend documentary, not the orchestra rehearsal, that is the subject of the film.

The orchestra rehearsal is designed for the television documentary filming it while the documentary has been designed for the film which films it. The orchestra rehearsal is a mock rehearsal and the television documentary filming it is a mock documentary.

Nothing represented in the film is exactly true. The falsity is asserted not denied. What Fellini shows is a duplicate of the real thing, its skewed copy. In part, this is a general condition of representation in the cinema. Film and photographic images represent what no longer exists. Fellini stages the no longer existing as having never really been. His film does not record a present or a past, it invents these. And it is the invention not the illusion that it might be true that is filmed.

Though this is a situation of all films, what makes Fellini's films different is the emphasis on distortion and the denial of a solid, realistic origin. What is filmed by Fellini may be real enough but the character of its reality is to emphasise that it has been staged, to appear not as real, as would be the case in most films, but as artificial.

Fellini introduces artifice within heterogeneous worlds on different planes, each modifying and sometimes denying the other. There is no unified centre. Even the most artificial of film genres, like the musical or horror, presents a world consistent in itself and homogeneous. Fellini does not do this.

Fellini can be linked to Renoir, who is realistic in the extreme and also theatrical, playing in the gap between them, their unresolvability.

There is no orchestra rehearsal in *Prova d'orchestra* except on the set.

The characters in the film make believe they are serious and that the apparent politics at play in the drama are serious, but none of this is marked as true no more than the documentary is to be taken as true. Every gesture is falsified by being excessive, magnified and exaggerated.

We are in a circus ring, not an oratorio, at a spectacle, not a rehearsal.

Similarly, usual notions of character are compromised. Insofar as the film is a documentary, the characters in it are persons, but the film of the documentary, which exists apart from it, reveals the documentary as false. Its characters can only be thought of as pretending to be what they appear.

Since falsity is the subject of the film and not only an instrument of it, the actors who make believe they are persons are also making believe they are actors in a documentary as if they are actors who are playing actors and actors who are playing characters as a consequence of them being in a documentary and in the parody–caricature of it at the same time.

They can never fully be themselves at any level and every role produces its parodic double.

Artificiality in Fellini's films is first of all not a consequence of filming but an effect of staging, an activity staged to be filmed and in such a way as to point to the deception of it as only being staged to be filmed even to the fact that the television camera is hidden, just like in a real documentary. There is no television camera, only a film camera, and that hidden, which evokes the (false) presence of the television camera, which does not exist and *therefore* cannot be seen.

Deception and its avowal are at the core of Fellini's films. The avowal of the deception is made evident by hyperbole and exaggeration in staging, costuming, lighting, music, performance such that every positive assertion is mocked as if by clowns in a circus. The delight of the films is not the illusions it creates but the illusions it reveals.

Every object and gesture veers toward a parody, amplified out of true, often by being made to appear even more true than the real thing, a super, hyperbolic real, as with Anita, for example, larger than life.

Fellini said that he thought the via Veneto he constructed in *La dolce vita* was more real than *the* via Veneto. Strolling on the real via Veneto, Fellini had the sense that it was the copy of the via Veneto he had made of it. The original was the artificial copy and the copy the real thing, like the painted moon in *E la nave va*, so real as to seem painted.

The reversal of original to copy is not simply a *tour de force* of artifice but a *tour de force* of artifice in the service of parody. There is no end to the spiral of artifice and copy in Fellini. It is a perfect labyrinth.

In Borges' story, *Pierre Menard, the Author of Don Quixote*, Menard rewrites *Don Quixote* exactly as it had been written.

Most film representation disavows its deceptions in the understatements of the true-seeming, the verisimilitude of the replica and the simulacrum, not Fellini's double, but rather the substitute.

Fellini's replica is a double laughingly pointing at its twin.

In *I clowns*, the real clowns who appear in it are never seen at work as clowns in an actual circus. The clowns are old, retired, and no longer perform. Fellini, interviews them 'off-stage' where they recall performances from their past. In one scene, a film record of a performance from the past burns through the celluloid when projected and disappears forever. None of this ever was and what disappears never existed. Yet, in the Fellini film of this never was, there is now a record of it having once been.

There is no true document, no true representation in Fellini's films.

The clowns who are no longer clowns perform as if they still are clowns while it is made clear that they are not. The doubling is a doubling of a once was as if it still is where the present recalls the past but falsely as reenactment. The funeral scene in *I clowns* is staged in the circus by circus clowns but they are placed there, staged for Fellini's false documentary as if what was taking place was taking place in the circus and at the same time not taking place in the circus but in its false reconstruction. A double of the false–true is staged and remains unresolved, infinitely divided.

Fellini's films have the successive structure of circus acts.

Each act is part of a sequential non-narrative. The successions are not consequences nor linked in a linear-causative chain familiar in the cinema. It often seems that another order would do instead of the one presented. Fellinian chronology has structured within it another chronology which would do just as well. The order of things is only hypothetical, not necessary. And the movement is circus-like and circular, serial returns.

I clowns is a condensed composite of other Fellini films which have a similar structure of buffoonery and self-mockery, the sequentiality of acts and the clowning around of clowns.

It is form that Fellini mocks.

Fellini's films laugh at themselves most when they pretend to be most realistic.

During a clown performance in *I clowns*, Fellini discusses clowning as the clowns are clowning about. A bucket, part of the clown act, then falls on Fellini's head, as if inadvertently, covering it, thereby dissolving the distinction between spectator and performer, film-maker and filmed. Fellini becomes a clown inside the performance of the clowns. He clowns in front of the camera like them and clowns with the camera in a receding, inclusive, dizzying see-saw of off-screen/on-stage.

The false belongs to the imaginary for Fellini. The false is true in spirit while the true is revealed as false. The cinéma vérité of documentary is foreign to the Fellini project which is founded on the delight of open artifice that is almost childlike. Documentary veracity is ridiculed as play, a form of inept artifice (what adults do) since no skill can make images into realities except that of the reality of the image and no event filmed is unequivocally real even if it is not staged and even if taken from 'real life'.

One of Fellini's earliest films, *Agenzia matrimoniale*, made for a cinéma vérité project of Cesare Zavattini, *L'amore in città*, intended to capture instances of reality, real moments of love in the city. *L'amore in città* was to be a magazine of life as it was being lived. In Zavattini's incident, *La storia di Caterina*, a woman who had abandoned her child, plays herself in the film. She duplicates her action of abandoning her child helped by all the actual persons who had been involved with her and who now act out their past involvement as it had been, thus exactly duplicating the real.

Zavattini's film is a serious experiment in truthfulness.

Zavattini wanted the experience of Caterina in reality to appear as accurately as possible on the screen. Instead, his episode in the film seems awkward and untrue.

Zavattini's film recalls, perversely, Welles' *The Immortal Story*, where the main character, the old merchant, Mr Clay, wants to turn a story which is not true into a reality in order that from henceforth the story which has never been anything but a story would become for the first time a story of the truth. He has various persons hired to enact the story and make it true, like a film director might. This quest for the true story is narrated by a narrator as if the story he is telling is true.

In the end Clay dies when the story is fulfilled in reality.

And that story of his quest and his death is the story that is told.

Fellini's episode in *L'amore in città* is not proposed as if it is true. It is presented as absurdly false (finding a wife for a werewolf), not a verisimilitude, but a false similitude which is easy enough to say but more difficult to express because a false similitude is a redundancy, exactly the character of Fellini's episode. By the fact that the episode is part of the film magazine of truths, it denies the truths of the other episodes or rather laughs at them. Fellini's story is absurd but the absurdity is a guide to a truth about stories and representing that makes the earnestness and truth of the Zavattini story seem impossibly false.

Fiction and documentary are usually contrasted. The one as make-believe and the other as reality. Fellini's films document the falsities of the real-seeming by the truths of artifice.

His films are false-true, a bucket over the head of the film-maker, a play with truth, not a resolution into truth.

SEE ALSO: WEREWOLF

Effacement

At the end of *I clowns*, as the White Clown calls up the memory of his Augusto Clown, Frou Frou, then conjures him up with a melancholy lament on a trumpet, and Frou Frou actually appears, out of memory, to become an image on the screen, at that moment, the present and past, actuality and memory, circus and documentary, living and dead, appear with him.

The White Clown with whom Fellini speaks, projects for Fellini another world, where Frou Frou and the White Clown can be together dancing to the music of their trumpets, cavorting in their happiness. It is a world that exists as desire, longing, memory and imagination. It is only visible in images on the screen as pure imagination and emotion.

The scene takes place underneath a Big Top tent empty but for the two clowns.

The colours are yellow and red bleeding into each other. Frou Frou is in black, the White Clown in white. The clowns dance their dance of love and friendship, the dance they once had danced in another world now passed. It is the dance they dance now in the blurred present where memory exists and which itself will pass.

That nether land is the cinema.

The clowns dance toward the exit of the circle. As they take their bows just before they take their leave they are wiped from the screen, effaced. A moment later the film comes to an end, itself effaced.

The dance that Ginger–Amelia–Giulietta and Fred–Pippo–Marcello dance in *Ginger e Fred* is a dance of parting in imitation of a dance by Rogers and Astaire where the two lovers also separate in another film.

The separation in *Ginger e Fred* reverberates through films, times, places and sentiments in which they are mediated and metamorphose.

There is the past of the time of Rogers and Astaire, the past of Ginger and

Fred who have come together from out of their past called into the present, where they do not belong, by television to do their dance and there is the past of Amelia and Pippo who had once been in love and who in the reality of their fiction as character–dancers imitating other character–dancers are still in love forced to part again as Ginger and Fred parted and Rogers and Astaire parted and Amelia and Fred had parted and as all the worlds they once belonged to passed. Finally, but not last, because these relations form a web of relations and a circle of relations, there is the past of Giulietta (Masina) and Marcello (Mastroianni) and Federico (Fellini), the roles they have played, the films they have shared, the past that has passed, all of their lives and all of their films, resurrected and saved in an instant, in the moment of their parting.

All of Fellini, the whole of the cinema, is compressed, expressed and projected there in a vertiginous overlay of shadows rescued from limbo where images abound and circulate waiting to be found again and summoned up.

When the television show in *Ginger e Fred* is over and the lights are extinguished, Amelia accompanies Pippo to the Stazione Termini in Rome which has been reconstructed on the set. They say their goodbyes. Pippo is at the entrance gate to the train. It is also the gate of their memories, former existences and love affair. An imaginary train whistle blows as it does in their dance on stage. For a split second Pippo returns to what he perhaps always was, Fred, and Amelia returns to what in her heart and passion she still is, Ginger. Their real selves are in their projected characters where they can dream and perform and dance.

These selves are what is most precious and fragile in them and which contain the memories, hence the images of their desires. The two characters disappear into nothingness which is where the sacred lives.

At that instant the film ends.

The clowns, Ginger and Fred, disappear having accomplished the impossible, recapturing an experience as it was at the moment it was experienced. This is only possible in film. The scene is a celebration and demonstration of the cinema's range, its power and its beauty.

During the dance of Ginger and Fred on the television stage, there is an electricity failure.

Pippo and Amelia sit at the edge of the stage waiting for power to be restored. In the darkness, Pippo whispers to Amelia: 'We are fantasms, we are fantasms that emerge from out of the darkness and disappear into the darkness.'

They decide to sneak away in the darkness, to say 'fuck you' to the sham and vulgarity. Suddenly power is restored. Their exit is illuminated. They have to return to the stage like naughty children having been caught. They complete their dance as Ginger and Fred.

The dance is stupendous.

In *Il Casanova di Federico Fellini*, the film has the scent of death. It is as if Casanova is walking through a world where everyone is no longer living yet nevertheless is present masked, costumed and in silhouette. Casanova too is made up, in masquerade, a fantasm in a universe of fantasms, there and absent.

The same perfume of death is present when Encolpio and Ascilto wander in the funereal landscape of *Fellini-Satyricon*, a film entirely devoted to the dead and apparitions of death.

These worlds are obliterated even as they are made present, more precisely, they are effaced in one world in order to be present and alive in another.

Effacement and death are the necessary conditions for the life of images.

SEE ALSO: CITATIONS, DANCE, MASTORNA

(The) Eye

An observation by Jean Clair: 'Le regard est l'érection de l'oeil'.

This is not an association nor a poetic metaphor. No likeness is assumed. Here, the look *is* the erection of the eye.

In some of Picasso's drawings, the opening of the erect penis is depicted as an eye. This relation is metaphoric.

The paint brush can be taken as an extension of the eye. To see and the desire to see and the will to represent what is seen has an erotic charge. When Picasso used his brush to paint a vulva or depict copulation, the association of erect penis and paint brush was more evident.

The brush of the paint brush is not unlike the curled hair of the pube.

The cinema for Fellini has four associations.

One, it is the feminine, of Woman, because it relates to fantasy. Woman, he says, is pure projection.

Two, the film theatre, where fantasies take place and are projected, is the womb. The entrance to it is the vagina, the succulence of the vaginal lips. In *Le tentazioni del Dottor Antonio*, there is an immense close-up of Anita Ekberg's mouth. To enter the theatre is to enter a woman, to surrender, happily, yet with a touch of fear and the excitement of anticipation, to viscosity, liquidity, milkiness.

Three, to film, to look, to see are erotic acts.

The camera eye for the film-maker, like the paint brush for the artist or the pen for the writer, is a sexual organ.

Four, the fantasmagoric dream images of the cinema can be images of death.

One week before Fellini began to shoot *Giulietta degli spiriti*, he dreamt that someone took out his right eye with a tablespoon. In the dream, Fellini experienced surprise but no pain. 'What did the dream mean?' he asked.

'Perhaps it meant', he said, 'that the film had no need of the right eye, but only required the left eye, the eye of the fantastic?'

This version of the story is Italian.

The same story in French adds that Fellini remarked that the left eye was the eye of fantasy and madness ('*fantaisie et folie*') and that the tablespoon had a knife-like edge. These remarks annotated a drawing made by Fellini of the dream scene in *Giulietta*. The drawing is an explicit reference to the cutting of the eye by the razor in Luis Buñuel's and Salvador Dalì's surrealist *Un chien andalou*.

The scene in *Un chien andalou* is associated with the cutting of the moon by a cloud. It brings into play lunacy, madness, milkiness, the vulva and the globular.

The razor and the cloud are both phallic.

In *E la nave va*, it is remarked of the rhinoceros whose milk saves Orlando when the *Gloria N* is sunk: 'Did you know that the rhinoceros gives excellent milk?'

It is not difficult to understand a set of associations in the dream which directly relates to Fellini's work.

The advantage of being blinded in the right eye of reason enables one to more readily enter a scene of fantasy controlled by the left eye of imagination where you see not outwardly, onto the world, but inwardly, into oneself. The inner place is the place of fantasy, culturally feminine not masculine, or perhaps, and more precisely, unsexed as angels and clowns are unsexed.

In the realm of sensuality and sexual indifference, blindness may not only be an advantage, but a positive pleasure.

Not to have a certain male sight, in effect, to be castrated, to lose sight, is to see things differently.

The camera is a curious phallic instrument since it is essentially a blind, dead eye. But then the eye of the penis does not see. It senses.

The deliciousness of filming as recording is not a passivity before reality, but a luxuriousness before unreality, before images which you project outwards through the eye of the camera from an interior which envelops you like the maternal womb. You project onto the world thereby recreating it by transforming it.

It is a creative eye.

To film is to reach this state like a dream.

It is said that Stan Brakhage filmed with his eyes closed to better see what was inside him. The eye was not the instrument which enabled you to see but a projector of internal visions best viewed with your eyes wide shut.

Blindness dictates a different way of going about things, a tentativeness, a feeling one's way, looking as a caress, fingers as eyes.

The inner eye transfigures, enabling a metamorphosis of reality. The objective, by being invested thereby with interiority, is invested with the spiritual.

Fellini's Casanova, and his Katzone, find their reason to exist solely as seducers of women. They catalogue, archive and celebrate their seductions. Women affirm the identity of the seducers by yielding to them. But seducers, affirmed by women, are also threatened by them and the forces of nature beyond their control which women unleash.

(This notion of the threatening female is turned into melodrama by Visconti: in *Rocco e i suoi fratelli*, for example.)

For the seducers and for all men, there will be a time when decay and impotence will take hold. The future of having no further future haunts Casanova from the beginning of the film, what Fellini called 'the vertigo of emptiness', an inability to penetrate into an inside, thereby a lack of intimacy and security.

I often have the impression with the absurd and grotesque scenes of sexuality in Fellini, that the object of love is not the excitement of passion but the security of returning to a mother.

It is not the past we must reckon with but the terror of the future. Hitchcockian anxiety is created in a future time.

The life of Casanova is a life of death and fear of it seen by his vitreous eye skimming the surfaces of reality.

When Fellini looked through the lens finder of the camera he saw his dreams and all the fantastic creatures his dreams gave rise to. The camera eye was like a window into another, richer world.

Casanova was essentially a voyeur and principally of himself. He saw nothing, created nothing.

To see properly you have to see inside yourself.

Fellini and Rossellini, like the Lumières, were intent on filming the invisible, the air, what Faure had said Velázquez painted. One sign of the modern in painting is a retreat from perspective and an advance toward immediacy and the tactile. The retinal irrational of the eye in Bataille's *Histoire de l'oeil*. His eye can smell, hear, taste.

And the eroticism of the voyeur, *flâneur*, seeking-out, penetrating Kino-Eye of Vertov's *The Man with a Movie Camera*: the feel of a stocking on flesh, of the weight and softness of a body by a bra being fastened, the impossibility of hiding from the intrusive eye, not a machine, but alive, full of desire.

Perspective is distancing, geometric and cool.

SEE ALSO: ANITA, GIULIETTA, ROSSELLINI

Fellini

Pasolini accompanied Fellini on evenings to the Rome *borgate* in search of locations for *Le notti di Cabiria*. Pasolini wrote a poem that refers to those excursions.

> With the tallest of these, I took the dark
> tunnel of the avenues, a night at the edges
> of the city trodden by lost souls,
> filthy crucifixes without thorns,
> joyful and fierce, thugs and whores,
> seized by anger in the gut, by joys
> light as the distant breezes
> gliding over them, over us, from the sea to the hills, in the time
> of nights that never die …

The evocation of Fellini and Pasolini in Pasolini's poem as they move through the *borgate* recalls Dante's *Inferno* and Cocteau's *Le Testament d'Orphée*.

It is an entry into another world, shadowy, unreal, across a divide. One poet, as if from the past (Pasolini–Virgil), is guiding the other, as if in the present (Fellini–Dante), into the world that is past but still exists in the present. The dead are still alive, perhaps more alive and palpable than those of this world, because they inhabit a world of images: 'those forms of existence, prey to a wind/that swept them along the ground/lifeless to death, unconscious to light …'

In the *borgate* Pasolini introduced Fellini to characters who Pasolini knows (they belong to a past Pasolini invented and resurrected) and who will become the characters in Fellini's *Le notti di Cabiria*.

Fellini in Pasolini's poem is like a character in Fellini's own films where

E la nave va: 'How marvellous! It seems almost false.'

E la nave va: Dorotea – like an angel.

E la nave va: the love sick rhinoceros.

E la nave va: Ziloev hypnotises a chicken.

Prova d'orchestra: the revolt of the players.

Prova d'orchestra: the destruction of the oratorio.

Prova d'orchestra: the conductor regains control.

Prova d'orchestra: harmony restored.

Giulietta degli spiriti: Giulietta plays with another identity.

Giulietta degli spiriti: Giulietta burning in hell in the school play.

Giulietta degli spiriti: Susy and Giulietta.

Giulietta degli spiriti: beach fashions.

Amarcord: Titta makes a pass at 'Gradisca' in the cinema.

Amarcord: the town comes out to greet Fascist officials.

Amarcord: the dream harem at the Grand Hotel.

Amarcord: the sighting of 'The Rex'.

Amarcord: Titta and the tobacconist.

Roma: the ecclesiastical fashion parade.

Roma: the ecclesiastical fashion parade.

Roma: whores on parade.

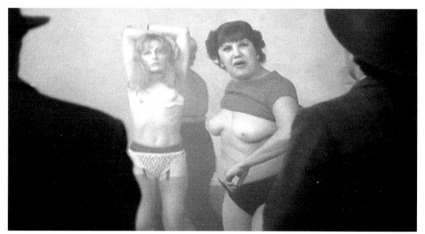

Roma: vanishing frescoes.

La città delle donne: Snàporaz in Katzone's gallery of women.

La città delle donne: little Snàporaz under a table looking under skirts.

La città delle donne: Snàporaz in the Luna Park of his memories.

he sometimes appears confronting his memories and their re-creations, seeing his own self and dreams.

Now he is a dream dreamt by Pasolini.

I have a sense about most films, the very best, and I feel it acutely with Fellini's, that they are a calling up from the depths, an entry and passage into the depths where the imaginary of oneself is more palpable and real than reality.

I have this sense too with the films of Orson Welles and of Nicholas Ray and it can be terrifying. In *Johnny Guitar* for example.

In the poem, a dark, oppressive dream world swirls around the poets. It is Pasolini's world, his invention. Fellini is an uneasy, uncertain, anxious spectator within it. The poem has assigned him this place. It is Pasolini's pleasure to do so.

I like films where characters are caught in other characters's stories into which they have been seduced and which they cannot comprehend, as in Welles' *The Immortal Story* and his *The Lady from Shanghai*, and also *Citizen Kane* where the character storytellers seek to enmesh Kane in their stories as the real story of Kane, but never succeed, and the plight of Joseph K in Welles' *The Trial*.

It can be terrifying. There is *Vertigo* of course. Rohmer does the same but gently.

Pasolini's work and this poem combine a rich citational poetry (the Bible, Dante, the Classical citations) with vulgar subjects (pimps, whores, thieves). The sub-proletariat *borgate* (low life) becomes the *Inferno* (high literature); the *Inferno* is brought low, resituated in the *borgate*. The one place contaminates the other and neither is what they completely are and yet they are by being placed by the side of what they are not.

The one is brought to heaven in words, the other brought back to earth by realities.

Pasolini plays with reversals. Each term, and the realities it signifies, becomes its opposite, while the oppositions still stand. Words become objects and objects thoughts. The *Inferno* and the *borgate* are opposed and reversible locations, but also terms, at once permeable to each other and irreconcilable opposites, a paradox.

Fellini conjoins the humble and the sublime often in the same being: Gelsomina, Cabiria, Zampanò. Or he conjoins opposites, as couples, at odds with each other: Gelsomina and Zampanò, Bario and Frou Frou, Ginger and Fred, the White Clown and the Augusto, order and anarchy, Cabiria and Oscar.

   Fellini's conjunctions are not antithetical, each is part of a unity. Pasolini dealt with irreconcilables, tension.

   Fellini's conjunctions are comparatively tranquil, gentle and easy.

The Fellinian method is parodic and caricatural, the exaggeration of the same, reflections in a distorting mirror of the fun fair. Ginger is the skewed image of Amelia, her other side, and Amelia the skewed image of Ginger, aspects of each other as Ginger is the complement of Fred and their dance an expression of a refound harmony that had been temporarily lost and dislocated. They discovered in the dance not simply each other but their own selves in the other.

   In the Fellini system differences illuminate each other, are reconciled. The system is composed of desires and dreams and creates a harmony.

Fellini felt out of place wandering with Pasolini in the *borgate*. He shyly, nervously ruffled his hair, spun the wheel of the Cadillac, an act of bravado: 'He drove his film producer-like Cadillac/with one finger, with the other, ruffling his young/large head, talking, tired and untiring …'

Fellini's *borgate* was not Pasolini's.

   In *Le notti di Cabiria*, Fellini turned Pasolini's hell into carnival, variety and circus. It is comic, sweet and filled with joy.

   Pasolini's love was an abstraction.

For Pasolini, Fellini's cinema was instinctive, part infantile and animal-like ('creaturale'), an instant inventiveness, unthought, interior and unconscious.

Fellini:

> I don't have the resources of critical distance that Pasolini possesses. Pasolini
> completely knows what he wants to do: he shoots a film and immediately
> after 'decodifies' it, as they say. I can't do this at all perhaps because I have a
> clandestine psychological relation with the cinema.

SEE ALSO: CLOWNS 2, (THE) SHERIFF, TRUMPETS

Giulietta

Fellini married Giulietta Masina in the autumn of 1943. The marriage lasted a lifetime. Fellini died in 1993 on their 50th wedding anniversary.

The characters Cico and Pallina were devised by Fellini for the popular humour magazine, *Marco Aurelio*, for which he had begun to write in 1938. The characters were adapted for the radio. Early in 1943, Masina interpreted the comic character of Pallina in a radio play. It was then that Fellini and Masina met.

Fellini's work on *Marco Aurelio* opened up possibilities for him as a scriptwriter. He worked as a scriptwriter for nearly a decade until he made his first film (with Alberto Lattuada), *Luci del varietà*, in 1950, in which Masina played the dutiful and neglected wife of the *capocomico* of the variety troupe. With the exception of her minor role as the prostitute Cabiria in *Lo sceicco bianco*, Masina, for Fellini, played the parts of wounded innocents, as wife, companion or lover in *La strada*, *Il bidone*, *Le notti di Cabiria*, *Giulietta degli spiriti*, *Ginger e Fred*.

Giulietta degli spiriti was made in 1965; *Ginger e Fred* in 1985.

Le notti di Cabiria: Cabiria after surviving a drowning by her pimp

In the role of wife, notably as 'Giulietta' in *Giulietta degli spiriti*, Masina is depicted as fussy, respectable, conventional, dull and unattractive. Jean-André Fieschi remarked at the time that her unattractiveness is so particular as to confer on the character of Giulietta a kind of beauty.

This beauty is strange.

In her roles as Gelsomina in *La strada* and Cabiria in *Le notti di Cabiria*, Masina is a clown-puppet, almost a painted figure, certainly traditional, with her wide eyes, grimaces, disjointedness, amazement, buffoonery, innocence.

As clown and wife, the characters are not erotic nor sexual.

They have a surreal aspect, even a disquieting one. It is more obvious when Masina is cast as a clown (*Cabiria*, *La strada*). In this role, she takes you by the hand into a world of magic, colour, enchantment, carnival that is ancient and to memory and childhood.

Masina as a wife is a wife excessively, to exasperation. The deformation explodes the conventions of the role and takes wifeliness outside the realities conferred on it by convention. Masina becomes an extra, super-ordinary wife, as if amazed at finding herself where she is. Wide-eyed she is as fantastic as when she is a clown.

This is the special beauty that Fieschi noticed, touched by innocence and magic and a sense of wonderment.

It is there when Gelsomina first sees Zampanò and then again when she

Le notti di Cabiria: Cabiria after surviving learning that Oscar was a fraud and intended to kill her

sees 'Il matto'. And it is there when Cabiria sees the fire eater in *Lo sceicco bianco* and as Cabiria again in *Le notti di Cabiria* when the movie star (Lazzari) who is a movie star (Nazzari) takes her to his fabulous house.

The colour and design of *Giulietta* is based on a comic strip. The character 'Giulietta' belongs to the caricatures of normality central to Fellini's work, exaggerating the normal until it passes into the other world of spectacle. Exaggeration is an instrument, like a secret formula, to facilitate the entry into make-believe.

There is a mocking quality to Masina's characters.

In the character of wife, the ordinary is in place at the outset, but becomes quickly out of place, at odds with itself, divided, an ill-adapted, uncomfortable ordinariness, and thereby special.

In the character of the clown, Masina plays an unreal figure victimised in the ordinary world because she is strange and innocent and vulnerable and does not belong. And she accuses the normal world of its normality and the hypocrisy of it, the make-believe of normality. The clown reveals something secret and inadmissable.

The Masina wives (Giulietta, Amelia) tend to liberate themselves from ordinariness by finding something else they had missed. The Masina clowns (Gelsomina, Cabiria) are made to suffer for their strangeness by being something other than is acceptable yet touching because they are in touch with dreams in their being, the dreams that others can only dream of.

In *Ginger e Fred*, Amelia, for a brief, exquisite moment, transforms herself into Ginger. Amelia who becomes Ginger accompanies Fred (Pippo) to the train station to say goodbye to him and to say goodbye to Ginger, her projected self that was part of their existence. Ginger was the self of Amelia's dreams. At the station, she becomes Amelia again, returns to reality, to the provinces, to marriage, all that Fellini fled from to go to Rome where he drew funny faces and wrote comic sketches, and entered the cinema as his other self, the clown, 'Fellini', belonging to a world of images, his masquerade and his true self.

SEE ALSO: FELLINI, PURITY, SPIRITS

Grace/grazia

I want to recall six scenes each of which conclude films by Fellini.

These scenes are scenes of grace.

They are redemptive and essentially sacred.

Fellini's characters are either anti-social clowns or conformist, socialised clowns. It is the anti-social he favours because it disrupts and disruption is an opening into the imaginary.

The anti-social characters are dishonest, destructive, mean, cruel. Often they are socially desituated: clowns, trapeze artists, mountebanks, hypnotists, travelling players, film-makers, actors, musicians, the mad, criminals, pranksters, tricksters. Such characters turn away from the social toward the fantastic, the infantile and the make-believe. These aspects are not separate.

Zampanò in *La strada* is all these things as is Augusto in *Il bidone*.

1. At the end of *La strada*, Zampanò is touched by grace at night on the beach before the vastness of the heavens and the stars. He breaks down in tears and agony.

2. At the moment before he dies, the soul of Augusto in *Il bidone* is stirred as he watches the peasants pass whose faggots on their backs make them seem like angels.

Do we see this objectively? Or has it been transfigured by Augusto's desperation? Or transfigured by our desires?

The soul of Zampanò had been similarly affected. The grace the two figures find is love, acceptance, recognition which comes upon them unheralded.

Grace finds you.

It is a scandal and tear in reality.

Grace is related to death and often met with at the moment of death as with Augusto.

It reminds me, though the register is different, of Pina meeting her death in Rossellini's *Paisà* and Edmund his death in Rossellini's *Germania, anno zero*.

Grace and reality are close to each other in Rossellini and also in Fellini. Grace is the grace of understanding. It occurs when reality, more precisely a secret in reality, reveals itself and in so doing the world and you are transformed. In Rossellini, reality finds you. Sometimes, when it does, it is a miracle. A similar sense of reality/grace occurs in Fellini.

It simply arrives.

Grace is a gift.

3. When all that is vile in the world has been revealed to Cabiria in *Le notti di Cabiria* and she is in complete despair, she recovers, smiles, joins the dance of the wandering young musicians on the road, returns to life.

4. Fausto, in *I vitelloni*, finally realises the awfulness of his conduct, his childishness, his destructiveness. He becomes, at least for the moment, different, grown-up, assumes his responsibilities as father and husband.

5. The chaos and utter ruin that the orchestra players experience at the end of *Prova d'orchestra* and which they have caused – the oratorio collapses, the world is turned to Hell, into dust, cacophony – call them back to an order and something more fine: to their instruments, to music, harmony, creativity, maturity, away from a Hell where they had been and had created as if possessed by the devil.

Though, it had been fun to be devilish. Fausto too had had his fun, and Zampanò, and Augusto do wicked, childish things.

The sources of creativity for Fellini reside here too. Devilish work can scandalise like grace can.

Prova d'orchestra is slapstick, circus clowning. It is like the Marx Brothers' film, *A Night at the Opera*. The Marx Brothers were delighted with the chaos they unleashed and the destruction they leave behind. These are the elements for another world.

Glee is *their* saving grace.

The scene in *Prova d'orchestra* when the dust settles and all goes quiet is like the penultimate scene of *I clowns*, the clown swishing through the silent air after the pandemonium of the mock clown funeral of Fischietto.

These scenes of harmony restored are not exactly self-realisations in the ordinary sense.

They are transformative and miraculous. It is not rational action nor consciousness that occurs, characters being brought to reason reasonably. It is more a metamorphosis, a spiritual transformation, being touched unaccountably that suddenly shifts everything.

These scenes are similar to the scene of the miracle in Rossellini's *Il Miracolo* and the monastery sequence in his *Paisà* both scripted by Fellini.

Is not Guido affected by a miracle at the end of *Otto e mezzo* when the film he has searched for and not found, comes to him from God knows where? Is not inspiration the arrival of grace? And is it not the artist then who receives the gift of creativity which comes if not from the heavens from a beyond?

There is a quality of resurrection and of salvation in Fellini, not necessarily religious, nor secular either. It is a bringing to the surface something hidden and precious often embodied in visions, dreams, memories, in images.

It is an understanding but one that is self-evident and does not require an explanation or interpretation being only what it is though never having been before. Fellini, like Rossellini, never argues.

6. The other scene I have in mind is a scene of the withholding of grace. It is in *La dolce vita* when Marcello, having seen the horror of the murder of Steiner's children and Steiner's suicide, can see nothing redemptive or beautiful any more, nor ever again. After a sad orgy of sex and drunkenness he comes on to a beach where Paola, with the face of innocence and the purity of an angel greets him. He does not recognise her.

Marcello has become immune to grace.

Grace is always present for Fellini, a quality in the universe, but not everyone is able to receive it or not all the time. You have to be open to it, even imagine it, or think it likely before it can arrive.

Bazin wrote about Fellini's films with unmatched acuity.

He noticed the lack of development in them, that events befall rather than develop. Fellini's structures are vertical, he said, that is, they are spiritual. The terrestrial is horizontal, logical, causative.

In the horizontal nothing comes unannounced. There is always a motive and an explanation and a preparation and thus every element is closely tied to every other. For grace to appear such tense linkages need to be loosened so there is a space for miracles and the self-evident which does not require intepretation.

Grace suggests a new narrative as in Fellini, as in Rossellini, and in Bresson.

Bazin also noticed that Fellini's characters do not change or mature. Instead, they are metamorphosed, a magical act.

And Bazin further noticed that the souls of Fellini's characters are either transparent, able to receive grace, like Zampanò or Augusto, or opaque, hard-hearted, unable to accept grace, like Marcello. Guido had to stop searching for inspiration to come to him. There are neither good nor bad characters, only those open or closed to grace.

There is no ethical, social or political system in Fellini's universe.

Clowns are true but they are not ethical.

Fellini deals in eternities.

Often, Fellini's characters who are in touch with the irrational and fantasy, like his clowns, lunatics, artists, whores, tricksters and children, are those to whom grace is given. Some glow with it like Dorotea on board the *Gloria N* and Aldina in *La voce della luna*.

Grace has a visionary, luminous quality. It is light and transfiguration. These are qualities of the moon and the cinema. The light of the moon is reflected and then projected.

The cinema projects and bathes all things in light, metamorphoses reality into the fantastic, thereby it touches the sacred.

SEE ALSO: ANGELS

Illusionism

The journalist Orlando, the character-narrator of *E la nave va*, tells the story of the funeral voyage of the liner the *Gloria N* as it occurs. He also exists at another time after the story has taken place. The voyage is at once in his present and in his past.

Another narrator, outside the film, narrates Orlando's narration and contains it. Orlando, as with character-narrators, is not omniscient and is often ignorant of events. There is much that he does not know and other stories escape him.

In addition, because his narrative is at two different times, the knowledge he has is at once limited to his present and retrospective. His narrative at the time of events is made to be the narrative of a reporter speaking to a camera recording what he says and recording the events he points to. The film, which stands outside Orlando's narration, records it and the documentary Orlando is making while throwing doubt on the veracity of everything or rather pointing to the artificiality of everything because the exterior film makes it clear that all you see and all that occurs has been staged including the documentary until what you see and take pleasure in is not the truth of things but their staging as make-believe.

The multiplicity and overlapping of times are vertiginous and also delightful. One time compromises and mocks the pretensions of another time and no time endures or is reliable and no place secure or dominant.

The labyrinth of times in *E la nave va* and in other Fellini films, the impossible times, is not simply a demonstration of disjunction and the play of it, or an entry into make-believe by means of exaggeration and the gaps it causes, it is also, by the fact of the cinema being so convincing in its constructions of the impossible, a testament to the power of cinema. It might seem an undue recollection, but it reminds me of Chris Marker's *La jetée* where Marker creates impossible unreconcilable times which you know to be impossible and yet these times on the screen are more than convincing; they are self-evidently right.

Orlando in *E la nave va* is intrusive, pathetic, incompetent, cloying, vain, unreliable and often drunk.

As in other Fellini films, the presence of a journalist, film crew, television crew, film set, television stage, rehearsal hall imply that the film you see is a document. At the same time it is revealed that the documentary is falsified. The events represented have been constructed and the recording of those events is equally constructed, the subject of another film, at another place and other time but going on at the same time in the same place. There are not fictional times and real times but different levels of fictional times some of which propose themselves as non-fictional but are in fact a fictional version of non-fiction.

There is no secure outside to a Fellini film which is not subject to the corrosiveness of time and the projections of desire, hence the lack of a centre, the certainty of a place and a defined punctual moment of beginnings.

Every beginning has already begun and that which is is often yet to be.

The voyage of the *Gloria N* in *E la nave va* fictitiously takes place in 1914. It is a comic book version of history. All that you see, the ocean liner, the sea, are painted, made of cardboard and plastic. To the fiction of the events is added the fiction that it is being recorded, reported at the same time and within the film, the events and the filming of them being contemporary. Hence, the film you see is not only a history of 1914, but part of the early history of the cinema when the actuality of voyages was the subject of the 'earliest' films which were geographical, ethnographic, concerned with travel and the exotic.

The voyager and the voyeur travel together.

When Jeanne Moreau takes her walk through Milan in Antonioni's *La notte*, she walks without purpose. The walk is a looking and we follow her with our eyes. The camera is our voyeur.

The 1914 film of the voyage of the *Gloria N*, silent and in sepia, becomes, within a few minutes of the opening of *E la nave va* a contemporary film in our present made in sound and in colour. The various times and gestures of *E la nave va* are sustained, run together and overlap. They are the true subject(s) of the film: the past events in 1914 (staged and invented), the documentary of these at the time (falsified), the memory of these events after their occurrence (faked), the filming which tells the story of these other stories and times, but is not above or completely outside them since every gesture is caught up within the make-believe and no truth or objectivity can survive this flux and absorption.

The *Gloria N* becomes involved in the events which lead to World War I. It rescues a group of Serbians in lifeboats. When challenged by an Austrian battleship, the *Gloria N* surrenders the Serbians to the Austrians. As the Serbians are being transported onto the Austrian battleship, one of them throws a bomb which blows up the Austrian ship. As it founders, it turns its guns on the *Gloria N*, sinking it.

Both ships are made of paint and cardboard.

The big guns of the Austrian battleship emit puffs of smoke as in a comic book drawing or one a child might make.

Orlando and a rhinoceros from the ship's hold are the only survivors of the *Gloria N*.

Orlando, ever the child, is sustained in his shipwreck by rhinoceros milk. Orlando continues his ludicrous narration from a lifeboat at whose prow lounges the rhinoceros who almost seems to be smiling. As he narrates an event which has occurred, it is being filmed by the documentary at the time of its occurrence and by the exterior film in the present of the filming. That all we see has already occurred is the sense of Orlando's narrative. That all we are seeing is now occurring is the sense of the documentary which records it which takes place within the film that frames it and is occurring now: three enunciating moments overlapping.

Orlando's narrative is composed of fact, memory, invention, misinformation and fancy. He colours his story to make it spectacular and more appealing, recalling events that never occurred or occurred differently than he reports and he invents as true what he does not know nor could have seen.

Orlando is an illusionist but not a good one, hence you see the deceits, but the deceits are endearing.

Much of what Orlando says, and that we see as a consequence, cannot be believed. We see events that may have only taken place in the mind of Orlando or are feigned to have taken place since Orlando is a charlatan. We see not the substance of things, but the imagining and imaging of them.

The narration lacks objective foundation.

The narration of Orlando's narration is as unreliable as Orlando's and equally, charmingly deceitful, because it is not dissembled.

The *Gloria N*, the funeral voyage, the absurd mourners are shadows called up from nowhere real. The shadows have been contrived, the non-existent given substance attesting not to the objects (an ocean liner, the passengers, the war, Orlando, the rhinoceros) but to their invention, and yet where, might it be asked, do these inventions come from? Where is nowhere?

The real in Fellini's films is a version of unreality. The illusions are illusions admitted as an aspect of the truth of the imaginary and of images. No reality is proposed as original. There are only instead differing multiple levels of unreality.

Fellini is a ringmaster of spectacles.

Orlando's reporting is mock reporting and his narration a mock memorial from a false present as the idea of the silent film being co-present with the voyage of the *Gloria N* is a fiction of co-presence. Orlando has one foot in the past (the fiction) and another in the present (the documentary as fiction) which the framing film exactly mirrors by its position which doubles that of Orlando and the documentary. Orlando's narration appears to issue from a fictitious present at the time of the events narrated while the present of today in the framing narrative is a present in which the past has been imagined and the imaginary then staged.

These various constructions however are shown to be constructions. There are no illusions which are not disillusioned.

The pleasure of the film is not to locate a truth or an illusory real but to see them in their contrivance.

At the end of the film, we are shown the set of the Fellini film, *E la nave va*, the film that we have just been watching, which is similar to the close of *Otto e mezzo* when the film doubles back on itself.

The finale of the film is this return, a finale that never ends.

On the set is a model of the *Gloria N* listing on a plastic sea, illuminated by a painted moon, rocked back and forth on a mechanical contraption, surrounded by technicians.

Fellini is on the set of *E la nave va* behind a camera, in yet another film, in yet another universe. Orlando is also on the set dressed like Fellini. They face each other reflected in a mirror each the distorted image of the other, like Guido and Fellini in *Otto e mezzo*, Fellini and Fellini in *Intervista* and Anita of *Intervista* regarding herself as Sylvia in *La dolce vita*.

In *Intervista*, Fellini is, like Orlando, the narrator and the object of a narration, a self doubled, not as in autobiography, still less as the truth of what you see, but as the reflection of what is seen, an image of an image.

In a Fellini film, it is difficult to say where staging begins and objectivity ends, or the reverse, when staging ends and objectivity begins. Everything is spectacle.

The set is the ship we sail on.

Fellini's work is not exactly a play with the relations of illusion to reality, fiction to truth, masquerade to the masked. His simulacra of the real, his images, are also the revelation that they are simulacra.

The naturalist shooting of the miracle of the children who sight the Virgin Mary in *La dolce vita* degenerates into absurdity. The absurdity is that of a false miracle (taken as actual) and the absurdity of a falsified naturalism that presents it as real. The television film crew and the reporters who follow the children in their dash to catch the shadow of the Virgin are tricksters to the television audience as the children are tricksters to their audience of believers wanting a miracle.

The arc lights, the storm, the chaos, the running about creates a fabulous spectacle of chaos within a false television report trying to cover it and itself included in the spectacle so covered, exactly what occurs in *Prova d'orchestra* and in *E la nave va*. Those who represent spectacle are, unknown to themselves, another spectacle to other spectators, who in turn … and so it goes unendingly.

There is no outside to Fellinian spectacle, no place that does not become spectacle, no place safe from fiction or mockery, no haven from duplication and from the absurdity of the attempt to make-believe that it is not a fiction we see composed of illusions and our desires, but a reality, out there, clear and unequivocal.

Fellini's models are the naive of the comic book, circus, circus clowns, variety theatre, Buster Keaton, Laurel and Hardy, the Marx Brothers. These unsettle and disturb. Clowning is a vision of fears, dreams, fantasies, savagery, stupidity, cruelty, a tender melancholy, the sadness of the trumpet, the fanfare, the marching.

Illusion is accorded an absurd joyous funeral at the end of the voyage of the *Gloria N*, a nostalgic farewell to a time when there was no difference between make-believe and reality, a time when Ginger danced with Fred.
    The time is the time of childhood.

SEE ALSO: DOCUMENTARY, ZOOLOGY

Love

Pasolini:

> Both Rossellini and Fellini, by the way they represent, by the way they shoot, have such an intensity of affection for the world as it is focussed by the eye of the camera, directly, obsessively, as to create, often magically, a three-dimensional sense of space (recall the sequence in which the *vitelloni* returning home at night kick a tin can): they are able to photograph even the air.

Pasolini's observation recalls Godard's quote in *Pierrot le fou* from the art historian, Élie Faure, about Velázquez that Belmondo reads in the bath to his little girl. Faure comments that Velázquez painted the invisible, that which lies between things, a silence from out of another universe.

Godard's interest in the gap between document and fiction, real and staged, reveals an ambition to represent the invisible. The oscillation between these conditions in his films is a method to reach the one by the other, recognising an absence in such a way as its presence can be felt and even seen though there is nothing there.

Il bidone: Augusto and his daughter

The ambition is indebted to Renoir and to Rossellini and to positions that belong to film realism.

Good film-makers and good painters film or paint the unseeable as good writers seek the unutterable.

The invisible in Fellini is evident in an unseen but sensed halo that forms around certain of his figures.

Cabiria has this halo as does the Franciscan friar she encounters in *Le notti di Cabiria*. The friar is played by the clown Polidor. It is not only the character who has the halo, but also the player. This halo, Pasolini observed, was a sign of love (grace).

Pasolini suggested a dialogue between Cabiria/Giulietta and the friar/Polidor where she would ask the friar where she might find grace. Polidor replies that perhaps she has no need of it.

Fellini decided not to use the scene, perhaps because the sense of it was already evident: Cabiria was filled with grace.

Polidor, the clown in *La dolce vita*, who is able to summon balloons with his trumpet, is in tune with a celestial, non-sexual love.

Music for Fellini comes from heaven. The trumpet is traditionally among the heavenly instruments. In Italy, trumpets unheard are blown by plaster angels on baroque and rococo church walls and painted onto the ceilings of cupolas.

La dolce vita: Marcello and Emma after her attempted suicide

Music from heaven is as unheard as the invisible painted by Velázquez.

In Marguerite Duras' *India Song*, the narrative told over the images is at a distance from what is seen. The characters are the shadows of themselves belonging elsewhere. The gap of image and sound is unbridgeable. It appears as if the present does not exist except as a place to recall images of the past but these images have no connection to the present. Thus the past though evoked in the present has itself no present into which it extends and the present that is evoked cannot reach a past to relate to.

The film is a pure film of time and its power is extraordinary.

Recently, I saw the film again and its mystery and force seemed even greater. Immediately afterwards, I saw Duras' *Son nom de Venise* which has the exact same soundtrack as *India Song*, but the images, until a brief wonderful moment at the end of the film, are images of emptiness, a ruined chateau, decay.

There are no characters, no figures, no action, no movement save that of the camera and there is the soundtrack from *India Song*. Connections are further strained than they are in *India Song*, more distanced, more obscure, sound and image further apart. The present is emptied out but so too is the past. All that remains are ghostly voices evocative of a past which cannot be seen and images of the ruin of the present.

It made me think of the depths of Welles' voices especially in *Kane*, rising up from the dead.

Though in this emptiness and dislocation you see less, sight is intensified but cannot be specified. Seeing is felt, a tactility. You see with your ears in deserted rooms, along surfaces of peeling walls, beside broken statuary accompanied by lengthy rhythmic tracks of the camera. Colours are reduced to pure matt tones in faded light dead yet reflective. As you see with your ears, you hear with your eyes.

India Song suddenly seemed overstated.

Pasolini: 'The real world is transfigured by the excess of love.'

See also: Angels, Grace, Rossellini, Trumpets

Lunatics

In *I clowns*, a group of clowns gives a performance for lunatics in an asylum. The clowns are suspended in the air costumed as butterflies and angels. They flap and wave about. Some play flutes and recorders. Others blow trumpets.

The lunatics are enthralled.

The clowns are not the only spectacle. The lunatics are also spectacle. As the clowns regard the lunatics who behave like clowns, the lunatics regard the clowns as among their own. We, the audience, belong to both and are also part of the spectacle.

The figures we regard as other are a part of ourselves.

Spectacle and spectator are interchangeable, serial, reversible, vertiginous.

Clowns, angels, lunatics emanate from worlds unknown. They are metaphors of each other, translatable, porous, permeable.

The unknown is an empty space. It states only itself, the lacunary.

The lacunary is created by a rupture in sense and control, an opening where significances can enter, but do not adhere.

Entry is temporary. The movement of sense, often a whirl, defers its own settlement. Deferral promotes odd encounters, unforeseen combinations, unheralded births, unsuspected becomings, the extraordinary, the wondrous, the miraculous.

This space is prolific, fertile.

It is the space of make-believe.

In Fellini's films there are many scenes of chaos and unhingings: *carnevale*, pandemonium, the party, the market, the railway station, the film set, the studio, the dance, the stage, the performance for lunatics, the circus, the beauty contest, the gnocchi festival, the pilgrimage, the miracle, the press conference, the striptease, weddings, public love-making, Bosch, the orchestra rehearsal.

Trumpets blow, drums pound, glass breaks, walls collapse, the earth quakes, as in Aristophanes' *The Frogs*.

There is shouting, tapping, clapping, streamers, to-ing, fro-ing, gobbling, farting, roarings, blows to the head, hysterical laughter, bands playing, cacophony, a letting loose, weird monsters appear from nowhere.

There is no hierarchy, subordination, order, instead criss-crossings, additions, overloadings, swellings.

Details accumulate, voices overlap, superimpose, centres multiply, exits and entrances proliferate, become each other.

At the interior of discord and disruption is the possibility of new patterns.

The existing order, *the* order is not satisfactory. Another order, not yet known, can be imagined, though not in detail, to accord better with our dreams and desires, an order of liberation. It is a disordered, other order. Hence, the preparations in Fellini's films, a kind of browsing patience for the liberating order to emerge: screen tests, interviews, the random search through photographs, backstage preparations, an expectation of something else, getting ready for it, for whatever might be before the curtain goes up, what might be formed out of the samples and variety of possibilities, waiting, being found by life or by death.

There is a reluctance to choose, to settle for something definite: Guido in *Otto e mezzo*, Fellini in *Intervista*.

Formlessness can bring forward who knows what and from where.

Formlessness is temporary and also continuous. Its disconnections and disaccords are opportunities for new combinations.

Ivo in *La voce della luna* hears voices from the bowels of the earth at the well.

From above, from the beyond, he hears the voice of the moon.

His eyes shine and glow in wonder and happiness.

Ivo is a clown like Gelsomina; he is a child like Cabiria; he is a madman alone in the midst of lunatics like Uncle Teo in *Amarcord*, up a tree, stoning his relatives, calling out for a woman: 'Voglio una donna!, Voglia una donna!', only allowing a dwarf nun to persuade him down from his tree.

Magical sounds fill the air for Ivo, murmurs tuned to the lunar (lunacy) and the infernal (chaos, terror).

Ivo is open to such sounds. The earth for him is a moonscape and he a Selenite. I thought of Georges Méliès and *Le Voyage sur la lune*.

One night during a full moon, his head filled with voices, whisperings, sighings, Ivo hears the murmur of men watching a no longer young woman, no longer beautiful, doing a clumsy, tacky striptease.

The men attack Ivo as an intruder.

To calm them and ingratiate himself, he tells them the story of Juno, the wife of Jupiter, the Queen of the Heavens. It is the story of the wondrousness of her milk spurting from her nipples to feed their child which forms the Milky Way, like the sparks of fireworks.

Where do the sparks go?

The flabby body of the woman and the goddess Juno are linked, a clown and a deity, the debased and the sublime, earth and heaven, the grotesque and the graceful.

Ivo's madness, innocence, infantilism can see such connections, effect such transformations, enabling one to transfer to another world, to the imaginary, to *Le voyage sur la lune*. The constant shift in all Fellini's films between a subjective and an objective view is the shifter into these transformations by way of projections. In the lunatic and the infant boundaries between interior and exterior are less firm.

This openness and sense of possibility is part of the modern.

La voce della luna is loosely based on Ermanno Cavazzoni's *Il poema dei lunatici*.

Madness, like clowning, is a mechanism to approach something otherwise inaccessible. (In Godard's *Pierrot le fou*, Pierrot brings together unlikely words and gestures, makes mad connections.)

Madness is a liberation from the usual constraints (social, ethical, cultural, linguistic), thus a pleasure and joy, a source of creation. Such liberation gives the mad (and the clown, the trickster and the artist) an advantage. It brings them toward a disengagement from life and in so doing closer to its poetry and beauty, hence closer to Fellini, who like Ivo, is a *lunatico*.

Bergson wrote of the necessary detachment of the artist from life.

In addition, perhaps, one needs a touch of madness.

Renoir's Boudu is a relative of Fellini's clowns as is Godard's Pierrot, Welles' Falstaff, Pasolini's Ninetto.

'Il matto' (the madman) in *La strada*, is a traditional figure from *commedia dell'arte* as is Zampanò and the pairing of Zampanò with 'Il matto'. These figures have another dimension, a sacred one, crucial for understanding the Fellinian connections between the unconscious, irrational, artistic, clownesque and the true.

> I believe in Jesus; he is not only the greatest character in the history of humanity but he continues to live as he who sacrifices himself for his neighbour.

The Madman is also Jesus.

SEE ALSO: CLOWNS 1, CLOWNS 2

Marcello/'Marcello'

'Marcello' is an important figure in Fellini's imaginary world.

Marcello has essentially three identities.

1. As the actor, Marcello Mastroianni;

2. As the character 'Marcello' (*La dolce vita*) or a character with a different name but nevertheless 'Marcello' (*Otto e mezzo*, *La città delle donne*, *Ginger e Fred*) and played by Mastroianni;

3. As the person Marcello Mastroianni playing himself (*Block-notes di un regista*, *Intervista*).

Mastroianni is present in all the variants of Marcello (Guido, Snàporaz, Pippo–Fred). He is not a character actor, nor a method actor, but plays

La dolce vita: Marcello and Sylvia

himself in various guises without being identified with any one identity in particular not even the one that is Mastroianni.

He is himself and not himself, a figure of fiction, an actor, and the person standing outside of himself looking in. He is in all these positions at once. 'Marcello' and Marcello are side by side, accompanying each other, reflecting one another, the self and its shadow, the one and its double. Marcello never completely enters artifice but never remains in a reality outside it except to point to the game, the play, the instability. But the pointing is part of the game and every outside in Fellini has another outside beyond it and so on.

'Marcello' seems often like a child wandering through a Luna Park which includes memories of childhood. As the character 'Marcello', he projects himself back into his imagined, fictional childhood when he was the child, 'Marcell(ino)'.

This happens in *Otto e mezzo*, *La dolce vita*, *La città delle donne*, *Ginger e Fred* and *Intervista*. Marcello as 'Marcello' or as Marcello by a different name, is the witness to his imagined self voyaging through the images in his mind played out as images on the screen.

In *La città delle donne*, Snàporaz–Marcello is in a fairy land of desire, infantilism and fear as surely as Jerry Lewis is in *Ladies' Man*.

The fairy land is regressive. Snàporaz enters it through a hole in a wall onto a slide, not unlike Alice through the looking glass.

The hole is vaginal, slippery, moist.

Snàporaz emerges sometime later as an adult or at least as more aware, regarding himself and his journey. This passage is repeated by Marcello in film after film. Grown but not adult, he returns to infancy to be reborn again by travelling back.

'Marcello' can and cannot be identified with Fellini.

He cannot be because the character of the one is differently located than the person of the other. This is true between Fellini and Mastroianni. It is also true because when Mastroianni is Fellini he is so at a distance.

It is Fellini projected, thrust forward and fictionalised.

On the other hand as Mastroianni is divided between Marcello/'Marcello' so too is Fellini divided between Fellini/'Fellini', one place of make-believe and another of awareness. It is the division and the impossibility of seizing upon it and possessing it as an identity that is duplicated between Fellini and Mastroianni. The film for Fellini is the voyage through fantasies and instincts as a voyage toward the sources of his creativity. Mastroianni is his vehicle and the film is also that vehicle and the consequence and evidence of the journey.

Almost every Fellini film from first to last is an entry into make-believe toward a consciousness of it in the facing of it and that consciousness is the film in its forms.

In *Block-notes di un regista*, *I clowns*, *Roma*, *Amarcord*, *Prova d'orchestra*, *E la nave va* and *Intervista*, Fellini plays himself as Mastroianni does as 'Marcello'. There are moments when Fellini encounters 'Fellini' and the two selves greet each other as Marcello comes across 'Marcello' on the set, like two symmetrical clowns in one body, distorted doubles of oneself, facing each other across a divide. It is welcoming oneself in a mirror and talking to oneself.

Together, often in one film, Fellini and Mastroianni are a couple, a *bande à part*. Or they are a couple simply because Mastroianni is Fellini's projection. Fellini is the chief of the band, but Mastroianni is his necessity. The relation is between a naughty self and an often distressed self (Marcello) who acts things out and a self who puts things in order (Fellini), sorting them to be properly presented. It is this process that is ingrained in the film, a process which reflects on itself and on film-making and therefore is always about the cinema, as all good films must be. The instruments of the cinema are not mere tools for Fellini, ways to express things, but the substance of his expression.

Part of that substance is called Marcello who is used by Fellini not to say something else but to say 'Marcello'. Mastroianni exemplifies the cinema of Fellini and the cinema of Fellini exemplifies the cinema. And that is why no matter how much it may appear that I am speaking about an *auteur* when I speak of Fellini, I am not, and Fellini is not an example of an *auteur*, except insofar as his films are reflections on film and take films in a new direction. It is the cinema that Fellini knows best and that constitutes the pleasure of his films. As Godard remarked, *la politique des auteurs*, was never about authorship.

Fellini spoke lovingly of Mastroianni's *disponibilità* (availability).

Disponibilità was the principal attribute for Fellini of a brilliant actor.

The brilliant actor was one open to the variations of imagined selves inside him, never completely himself but never purely fictional, oneself and other than oneself simultaneously, in dialogue and in play and able to be projected.

Marcello as Mandrake performed magic tricks that were false. The play of falsity and truth was the delight of his performances, a lightness of touch, a not taking oneself too seriously, being in two places at once, a caricature and a self-effacement, an exaggeration of self and an intense modesty.

Marcello, for Fellini, was among the aristocrats of his profession, that is, among the clowns.

SEE ALSO: CLOWNS 1, GIULIETTA, MASTORNA

Mastorna

In 1965–66 Fellini wrote the script for a film called *Il viaggio di G. Mastorna* (*The Voyage of G. Mastorna*). It was to be produced by Dino De Laurentiis. For various reasons the film was never made.

The full name of the principal character was Guido Mastorna. 'Mastorna' is a play on 'Mas'troianni and ri'torna', thus, 'Mastroianni returns'. Guido is the name of the film director in *Otto e mezzo* interpreted by Marcello Mastroianni. Guido Mastorna – Mastroianni returned or resurrected – is the conductor of an orchestra. There is an orchestra conductor in *Prova d'orchestra* played by Baldwin Baas.

Guido, in *Otto e mezzo*, inhabits two worlds.

One is fictional-real and part of the everyday and the other made of his dreams and memories of which the audience has a privileged view. At the end of the film, Guido transports his dreams back to the real world where he makes a film of them, a film we have already seen, *Otto e mezzo*. It is as if the reality that we have seen has been in part a dream and the film the trace of that dream. *Otto e mezzo* is the film to be made at the close of *Otto e mezzo* and is the duplicate of the *Otto e mezzo* that has been made and already seen (by the audience).

At the opening of *Il viaggio di G. Mastorna*, Mastorna has just died in a plane crash. The world of the dead in which he wanders is like the world of the living he has come from but with an indefinable difference which he notices without comprehending. Mastorna, in the world of the dead, believes himself still to be among the living. It is because the world of the dead is a duplicate shadow world of the world of the living.

Death is a parody of life, the final joke.

Mastorna is a spectator in a shadow world of images, watching what no longer is, including watching himself who has passed to the beyond where he is living and not living. Mastorna has been resurrected … as an image.

The grotesque in *Mastorna* is grotesque because in every respect death is made to seem like life (as films are made to seem real). Death appears as a perversely normal living not particularly exaggerated nor markedly different. The slightness of the difference is the joke and the exaggeration. It is not unlike the funeral of Fischietto the clown in *I clowns* where clowns treat the funeral of a clown as an opportunity to clown about and mourn grotesquely.

In the script, it takes Mastorna some time to realise he is dead.

At the end of the story, Mastorna enters a city which looks exactly like Florence.

It is Florence in all particulars: the streets, sunlight, buildings, shops, flower sellers, traffic lights, smells. Yet, it is as if Mastorna is seeing a Florence which he has always known, but which is indefinably different.

The difference is that he is dead and that the Florence he wanders in is an underworld reflection of 'Florence' like the via Veneto Fellini constructs on the set in *La dolce vita*. It is almost the same as the real thing.

Mastorna enters a theatre, takes his place in the orchestra pit, waves to his wife whom he sees in the audience, raises his baton, brings it into play and the music of the orchestra begins.

The music is rich and solemn, grandiose and grave, sweet and intoxicating, sounds from another world, like the voice of the moon.

SEE ALSO: EFFACEMENT, LUNATICS

Oxymoron

Giulietta Masina plays the whore Cabiria in *Lo sceicco bianco* and in *Le notti di Cabiria*. The role seems ill-adapted to her person physically, to her manner and to her dress. She is small, neither boy nor girl, slightly deranged, with the movements of a puppet, wears dresses with horizontal stripes, loses interest in a client in order to watch instead, enraptured, a fire-eater. Cabiria is not sexy, nor tarty nor seductive.

Fellini said that Giulietta as Cabiria and as Gelsomina (in *La strada*) is a clown. Clowns, he said, are without sex, like Laurel and Hardy (who usually slept together) or Charlie Chaplin, or angels, or Totò. It is a quality of child-likeness

Cabiria is an oxymoron, her own antithesis.

Fellini's films are filled with self-contradictory figures.

Sylvia (Anita Ekberg), dressed in the costume of a cleric, walks up the

La dolce vita: Marcello with Sylvia dressed as a priest

interior staircase at St Peter's followed by Marcello, panting and desirous. On the terrace, high up in the tower, above the square, she loses her wide-brimmed clerical hat to the wind.

Anita as a cleric is absurd.

In *Il bidone*, Augusto (Broderick Crawford), rough, with a raspy voice, tired and melancholy, bearing the scars from other films where he was a gangster and a demagogue is a swindler and confidence trickster. One scam in the film (repeated twice) requires him to dress and act like a Vatican bishop. The role and the costume mock him, negate him, as Anita is mocked by her clerical costume. These parodies also work in reverse: gangsters are ridiculed for appearing as bishops and bishops ridiculed by the gangsters impersonating them.

Since Fellini never effaces actors by the characters they play a further dimension of mockery is introduced. Crawford as a bishop is absurd because of his manner and appearance and because these qualities identified him as a gangster in other films. The make-believe of cinema is not called in doubt here by mockery but celebrated.

Otto e mezzo: Carla the housewife as whore with Guido at the spa

But of course!

Monsignore Augusto. Padre Anita.

It is very silly.

In *E la nave va*, the Grand Duke of Austria is played by a chubby actor (Fiorenzo Serra) who seems to be a woman in drag. Also in the film, the ghost of Edmea Tetua makes a sudden entry into the midst of a séance organised to summon her from the dead. She is played (impersonated) by a young man of uncertain sexuality who adores the dead Edmea whom he becomes (impersonates) for a practical joke.

Are not all of the characters in the film impersonating the dead?

E la nave va is an 'historical' film impersonating the historical real. It constitutes an overwhelming exaggerated redundancy.

One of the young boys in *Intervista* is a young woman. There are hermaphrodites and transvestites in *La dolce vita*, *Fellini-Satyricon*, *Roma*, *Il Casanova di Federico Fellini*, *La città delle donne*, *Ginger e Fred*.

The costumes, impersonations and the living–dead, all preposterous and sometimes grotesque, nevertheless, have their appeal.

These antitheses can approach the monstrous.

In *Fellini-Satyricon* there is the light-sensitive, heat-sensitive, half-human, half-god, albino hermaphrodite, viscous like milk, disgusting as it disintegrates. Regarding is touching it. The screen oozes. And in the same film there is a minotaur.

In *Intervista*, a Communist plays at being a Fascist as girls play at being boys and no one is as they seem to be, including Fellini, a fake film director/a real film director. The masquerades are transparent. Every gesture which feigns is pointed to and laughed at. It is the absurdity that is the fascination and the fun.

At the New Year's Eve Ball in *I vitelloni*, Riccardo is dressed as a medieval cavalier, Leopoldo as a Chinaman, Alberto as a woman, Moraldo as a sailor. Casanova in *Il Casanova* is permanently in costume and his looks distorted by elaborate make-up, a distortion not designed to make Donald Sutherland the likeness of Casanova but to make Sutherland the distortion of the likeness, a caricature. Sutherland is not effaced, on the contrary.

Dressing up to be who you are not in Fellini's films goes along with his monsters, hermaphrodites and transvestites.

Three examples will serve.

1. In *Roma*, there is an ecclesiastical fashion parade. The ecclesiastics who watch it, including a cardinal, are dressed appropriately as ecclesiastics and act accordingly. The spectacle and costumes of the show mock the spectacle and costumes of the audience. The mirror is contradictory undermining the stability, place or origin of either performers or audience.

Which is the reflection? Which the masquerade? Which the theatre? Where the fashion parade?

The same questions could be asked of *Prova d'orchestra* where everything is faked but nothing hidden.

There is no stability in the comparisons and contrasts in the ecclesiastical fashion parade. Movement is from one to the other, spectator to performers, then back again without a firm referent to return to. It is circular, going nowhere, its signifiers lacking referents to which they can unequivocally attach which extends the range and possibilities of attachments. It liberates the signifiers and enlivens them.

2. In *Ginger e Fred*, there is a parade of lookalikes at odds with themselves not unlike the Siamese twins in formaldehyde in *I clowns*. The lookalikes are of Marcel Proust, Clark Gable, Queen Elizabeth II of England, Ronald Reagan, JR (from *Dallas*), Woody Allen, Pius XII, Marlene Dietrich and Bette Davis.

3. In *Lo sceicco bianco*, Wanda (Brunella Bovo) thinks herself to be the character of the slave girl in the photo-romance, *The White Sheik*. She falls in love with the white sheik, Fernando Rivoli (Alberto Sordi), who in reality is a pathetic seducer, a hen-pecked husband, and an endearing liar.

Wanda enters the world of the photo-romance where she is the contrary of who she really is, like Rivoli is, like all the characters are. The characters are not who they make themselves up to be yet act as if they are: the white sheik (Rivoli) tries to seduce the slave girl (Wanda) only to be thwarted when Wanda wakes from her dream, becomes herself again, and Rivoli's wife waits for him on shore, ready to pounce.

Characters resemble themselves and negate themselves. It constitutes a closed circle of antithetical contrary identities that nevertheless call to each other as related.

Alberto Sordi, the actor, enters the circle as a further term in *Lo sceicco bianco*. Sordi impersonates Rivoli who impersonates the white sheik, each projecting upon the other their inventive childlikeness and clowning.

To falsify a representation is to loosen the hold of reality. It strengthens the status of what is seen as an image with its own power and not derived from what it represents. The power of the image is in its fluidity, its ability to migrate to unseen places, attach itself to unforeseen images and be declined within new associative fields.

Reality as representation is thereby left behind and film in its forms, images as images, reinstated.

The antitheses central to these divided figures and what constitutes their essential structure and composition make reality equivocal.

Equivocation sustains a world of images, resemblances, make-believe against the apparent resistance of reality. Reality is no longer opaque and solid but diaphanous and fragile. It is the world of images Wanda enters into because that world is permeable, multiple, made of superimposed levels without hierarchy of fixity, and because of this openness, the lack of restriction, it is tempting.

Equivocation enables. It helps create a flow of images and associations, of 'acts', spectacles, of colour and light and chaos and explosions none of which can be exactly predicted in advance whereas a close narrative of events, by its inexorable consequences and effects, disenables, tightens, limits.

Equivocation sustains liquidity and the life of film.

SEE ALSO: ILLUSIONISM

Purity

Is it possible to film purity in the cinema? Pure love?

It is easier to film a battle scene, said Godard.

Deceit is at the heart of the cinema. To seek truth in images, to find in them sincerity and reality, would be to somehow get beyond the fakery of representation. One way to counter deceit is to avoid all that might be thought of as interpretation. In effect, to avoid perspective, connectives, hierarchies, to be blank in the face of reality.

Eric Rohmer objectively follows his characters. The characters however look at themselves and others with self-interest, that is, not objectively. They create fictions out of what they find and from what is presented to them. Rohmer records what they create, having given them the opportunity.

Otto e mezzo: 'Claudia'

Rohmer's films are fictions and they are not. The story of Rohmer's films is the story of the fictionalisations created by his characters that Rohmer films as if he is not himself presenting a fiction, but only recording fictions.

The effort required not to adorn reality is considerable. Bresson perhaps has been the most successful.

Rossellini stripped reality of its accretions in order to get close to it. Fellini exaggerates and falsifies reality, excessively fabricates it, over-elaborates it, as a mockery of it. The parody creates distances but is not a view. His devices avoid, repel, distort, not by backing off, but by coming too close as with a magnifying lens.

Rather than seeking sincerity, Fellini denounces the false sincerity of representation in order that sincerity might be better preserved. To openly falsify to him is more honest than to create an illusion as if you are not falsifying.

Scenes of sex in Fellini's films are shams and grotesques. They declare that they are faked, mere performances. Fellinian sex is hyperbole, falsification, monstrousness, childishness, infantile vileness (Fausto in *I vitelloni*, Casanova, Katzone in *La città delle donne*). It de-eroticises laughingly.

Sex is simulated to represent not sex but the act of simulated sex, the double of sex. It points to itself as fabrication.

Casanova in *Il Casanova* makes love obsessively, has women infinitely, sweats copiously, groans noisily, but he is sexless, unerotic. His performances are purely literary, to be catalogued and recorded. Casanova does not make love but mimics making love. He accumulates such scenes like Katzone and his 10,000 conquests.

Casanova is a sad clown clowning it up as a Casanova.

In the last 'act' of the film, Casanova dances, and with the solemn gestures of desire and passion, with a mechanical doll with red porcelain cheeks and wide eyes, expressionless except for desires you might project on her.

This doll is not a doll, but a woman making believe she is a doll.

Purity is sustained in Fellini's work by intimating that it is elsewhere than where it can be represented. Fellini refuses the attempt to represent sincerity because he deems it impossible in advance.

Sincerity is there or it is not, self-evident or not. It cannot be explained, interpreted, represented.

Only clowns are the defenders of purity.

SEE ALSO: DOCUMENTARY, ROSSELLINI

Rimini I

Fellini was born in 1920 in Rimini where he grew up. Rimini is a small town on the Adriatic coast. In the summer it is a bathing resort.

In 1938, Fellini left Rimini for Rome, ostensibly to enrol at university to study law. Instead, he went the rounds of various weekly, bi-monthly and monthly magazines to see if he could find work writing comic sketches, caricatures, short stories.

He was successful and came to write for nearly a dozen popular magazines, for radio and for variety comedians, like Aldo Fabrizi, the priest in Rossellini's *Roma città aperta*. Eventually, Fellini began writing for the cinema with the help of Fabrizi.

He loved his new life.

Twelve of Fellini's 24 films are set in Rome, actual or fabricated. Seven of his films are set in the provinces, real in his early period (*I vitelloni*),

Otto e mezzo: Saraghina and little Guido and his schoolmates

created on the set in his later work (*Amarcord*). Some of these provincial settings are in towns along the Adriatic, like Rimini. Journeys from the provinces to Rome occur in 14 of his films, notably in *Lo sceicco bianco*, *I vitelloni*, *Roma* and *Intervista*.

Memory is vertical and atemporal. You remember the past in the present as if you are in two places simultaneously, one remembered, the other from which you remember as in the gap between an enunciated and its enunciation.

Memory does not always look back. It can look forward which causes a projection of the future into the past as if the future is in the past. Much of what is remembered is contrived to appear as memory but is often only a story we tell ourselves. Stories narrated as memory may never have occurred, in fact this is usually the case.

The fabricated memories in Fellini's films are false in relation to a true course of events, but true as desire. For example, Fellini's story that he ran away to the circus. He did not run away to the circus, but then he did as well.

Memory can disguise a forgetting or distort a truth. Memory itself can be remembered or feigned as if you remembered it as you can be nostalgic about a nostalgia you never felt but would have liked to have felt or are convinced that you felt.

Fellini's Casanova remembers his life and relates (invents) the memory of it as a narrative. His memory is a story.

Marcello, Anita and Fellini remember aspects of their lives in *Intervista*. What they remember is their films. This memory is called up as fragments in images from films in the past (*La dolce vita*) which the actors regard from the present of *Intervista*. They are remembering what is already memorialised and that permits them, because it is on film and memorialised, to have their memory actually present with them. The past and present appear simultaneously in a single image containing a double image of the past and the present looking at each other.

Orlando remembers the voyage of the *Gloria N* in *E la nave va*, but nothing of what he says he remembers as ever having occurred. He has invented everything including his fictitious self for the sake of a story to tell and in which he is its hero and survivor. To exist at all, Orlando requires a memory to define himself and thus finds a memory in a narrative to bring himself to life, a contrived past providing him with a contrived present.

Fellini remembers the circus of his childhood in *I clowns* and he recalls the Rome of his youth in *Roma*. What is interesting is less what is remembered than the contrivance of the memory, the fabricated circus of memory, the resurrected clowns of memory, the constructed Rome of memory. Fellini does not remember and represent the memory. He constructs memory as if it is memory. It is this activity of enunciating that is fascinating and delightful, memory as a spectacle staged.

Amelia and Pippo remember their past as 'Ginger and Fred' whose memory they reenact and bring to 'life' in dance. They are their own instruments of projection, by their bodies and their voices, to impersonate their past as images and as memories come to life. The coming to life is also a return to memories.

The coming to life can only be an image.

In *Amarcord*, one of the main characters in a cast of clowns is Gradisca who excites all the men in the town especially the young ones. She is a figure created by adolescent dreams, an image not a person. *Amarcord* is a concocted memory of the provinces and she is a crucial ingredient of the concoction.

One scene relates how 'Gradisca', ('Please accept' or 'Have a taste') acquired her name. A gorgeous fairy prince visits Rimini. Gradisca lies in a veiled bed in a pink-hued room, naked, flushed pink with desire, waiting for him. He parts the veil, she opens herself to the prince, like a box of chocolates, and she sighs, 'Gradisca'.

The story, Fellini said, belongs to his past in Rimini.

When he was an adolescent in Rimini, the scent and sight of the 'real'

Gradisca made him tremble with longing and the impossibility of realising his desires.

Fellini and his friends regarded what they could not have. He remembers their role as spectators of unrequited desires which Fellini reenacts in the film: the seductions they saw at the Grand Hotel, the fabulous princes who came with their concubines, the fleshiness of Gradisca.

Fellini often reenacts dreams of potency which end in failure not because that happened but because disproportion and mockery are the motives and subjects of his creations.

Fellini relates:

> Traumatised, … by that memory; many years later I went into the fields of Comasco in search of Gradisca; I had been told that she had married a sailor cousin and I wanted to see her again. I took the Jaguar into a wretched village, in a muddy delta. There was an old woman hanging out her clothes in the garden. 'Excuse me', I asked her, 'do you know where Gradisca lives?' 'Who wants her?', the old woman responded. 'I'm an acquaintance. Do you know where she is?' 'It's me', said the old woman.
>
> That was Gradisca. She had lost all trace, even the faintest, of her triumphant carnivalesque sparkle. I made a few calculations. Thinking about it, it had to be right, she had to be 60.

This entire scene is repeated in Fellini's relation of how he trembled with shyness when he first met Anita Ekberg in her hotel room. And it is repeated again in the Fontana di Trevi scene between Sylvia and Marcello. And the conclusion of the Gradisca story is also concluded in the presence of Anita in *Intervista* gazing at the Anita she once was in *La dolce vita* to make men gasp with desire.

SEE ALSO: ANITA

Rimini 2

Much of *Lo sceicco bianco* was shot on the beach at Ostia, just outside Rome.

Ostia was the main port of Rome in ancient times. There are ruins at Ostia of classical Ostia.

Just beside Ostia is Fregene, an enclave of the rich on the beach front in a pine forest. Fellini and Masina had a house there in addition to their flat in Rome. Most of *Giulietta degli spiriti* is shot in Fregene.

Beaches are important locations in Fellini's films: in *Lo sceicco bianco, I vitelloni, La strada, La dolce vita, Otto e mezzo, Giulietta degli spiriti, Amarcord, Fellini-Satyricon*. The beach is a remembered place or a place that provokes characters to remember. It is also a place where memory may be blocked as at the beginning of *Otto e mezzo* where Guido dreams first of being confined in his car in a traffic jam and then hauled down to earth on a beach as he flies through the air.

The beach has a sense in Fellini's films of something wonderful and unattainable, as if it is a sign of memory itself and also a place of desolation and emptiness.

Amarcord, made in 1973 in colour, reconstructs an imaginary Rimini on the set in Cinecittà in Rome. *I vitelloni*, made in 1953 in black-and-white, also takes place in an imaginary Rimini shot in the real Ostia.

Ostia *is* Rimini in the film.

In the one instance, Rimini is fabricated, in the other it is projected upon another, similar reality.

Fellini related that one day, at Ostia, the pounding of the black sea and its smells evoked in him a nostalgia for Rimini.

An overlap of times overlapped place.

After leaving Rimini in late adolescence, Fellini seldom returned. He had escaped Rimini to be in Rome and to be free, where it was possible to dream uncensored dreams and to make dreams come true by constructing them on the set and in images in films. To be a film-maker was never to leave your dreams behind. It was to have them safely and permanently, in effect, to live with them. Rome and the cinema were these places of dreams and images.

In Rimini, making dreams come true was not possible because the only dream you could have in Rimini was not to be there. The Rimini dream was the dream of Rome. And only in Rome, a Rome that never ceased being a dreamt spectacle for Fellini, could you dream the dream of Rimini.

And what was that dream? It was the dream to be elsewhere. It is what Fellini dreams in the Riminis he invents. It is the dream of a provincial wanting to flee the provinces.

In Rome, at Cinecittà, at Ostia, Fellini could dream without fear of being censored.

By the side of Fellini's Rome was Fellini's Rimini (*Mia Rimini*, *My Rimini*, he wrote), but cleansed of its *humeurs viscérales*, of its reality.

It was not true, as Fellini said it was, that there was no difference for him between reality and what you imagined it to be. The difference was crucial.

It was the difference that *told*.

SEE ALSO: RUBINI

Rossellini 1

Rossellini said, 'Reality is there, why manipulate it?'

Fellini said that Rossellini photographed things and the air around them, 'to reveal what is elusive, mysterious …'

The Lumière film *Le Repas de bébé* was screened in the first Lumière programme in Paris in 1895. In it, Auguste Lumière feeds his baby daughter. In the background the leaves of a hedge flutter in a soft breeze. Sunlight shimmers on the surface of the leaves as in an Impressionist painting.

This atmosphere and its details are compelling.

Ferdinand/Pierrot/Belmondo in Godard's *Pierrot le fou* reads to his small daughter a passage in a book by the art historian Élie Faure. Belmondo is in the bath and the little girl is standing beside him.

> Velázquez, after fifty years, no longer ever painted precise things. He wandered around objects as with the air and the dusk … in the shadows and from the clearness of the depths, he caught the brightly coloured quiverings at the invisible centre of his silent symphony. He no longer engaged with the world.
>
> … the mysterious exchanges that penetrate forms and tones the one with the other, by a secret and continuous movement in which no noise, no violent start betrays or interrupts the progress. Space rules …
>
> It is like an aerial wave that glides on surfaces, filling itself with their invisible odours in order to define and shape them, and to transport them everywhere elsewhere like a scent, like an echo dispersed on the entire extent of the surroundings in imponderable dust.

Faure wrote in the 1920s. Godard approves of the citation. It accords with his own view of cinema, its links to painting and its modernism. It echoes Fellini's remarks about Rossellini. Rossellini was one of Godard's heroes and reference points for everything the cinema could be and ought to be.

Rossellini travelled throughout Italy in 1946 to make *Paisà* accompanied by Fellini who loved the experience, the sense of making a film as an activity that was part of life and that sought out the life around the filming and made it part of the film.

Life as a film. A Fellini ideal.

For Fellini the casualness and joy of the experience with Rossellini was a liberation.

Paisà begins in Sicily in 1943 and closes in the Po Valley in 1944 just before the end of the war in Italy. It follows the pattern of war as it moved from the Italian south to the north after the Allied landings. There are six episodes in the film: in Sicily, Naples, Rome, Florence, Emilia Romagna and the Po Valley.

Fellini scripted, and may have partly shot, the fifth episode at a Franciscan monastery in Emilia Romagna.

The episodes are separate and disconnected. There is no continuity between them though there is a stylistic unity and the fact of the overall progress of the war. At the end of each episode something that was present but invisible in each of them is suddenly, often painfully revealed. The revelations are variously scandalous, mysterious or miraculous. In any case, a disruption not simply of what is there but what has not been seen, a disruption in consciousness and understanding for the characters in the episodes and we who have been watching them. It overturns everything.

Hidden within reality is the enigma of it. The presence of the enigma takes us unaware and confronts us in a turn of events.

Each episode in *Paisà* is plain, direct, distanced, spontaneous, made with an apparent indifference. The filming and acting are awkward and clumsy. There is no search for the beautiful image. When scandal arrives or the miraculous takes place, it does so unemphatically and unannounced. Everything was one thing, then it was another. 'Then' marks out a succession but not a logic. What occurs is part of the scheme of things. All things in the scheme are simply there, unweighted and equal.

The episodes move to a conclusion without, it seems, knowing in advance what the conclusion will be. The film does not accumulate. It subtracts. Each step forward erases the previous step while the surface registers neither consequence nor effect. Only the facts are given: blank, opaque, resisting interpretation. Reality is framed without a conclusion being drawn. The usual narrative procedures of motive and consequence, logic and consistency are absent, hence too significance as something given in advance.

Reality is simply 'there' though not by that fact self-evident. It would be wrong if the film gave to reality what it did not possess.

Something is happening, at the inside, at the surrounds, in the air and at a depth, but it is unseen. The film points to nothing only showing what it finds and has been presented to it.

Rossellini is always discreet.

'Why manipulate reality?' is a refusal to unify, interpret, weigh, demonstrate. Instead, Rossellini shows, reluctant to dissolve what he regards as the mystery of the real. The self-evident is not the explicable but the existent, the what is there.

When the hidden makes itself felt, it is sudden, often violent, like a gunshot. It 'comes', shuddering into being and nothing is quite ever the same again. The difference is not a matter of words or explanations but of experience, of showing, seeing. You cannot summarise such difference or translate it into words. What is given is a recognition which is sensual, physical, tactile, a different manner of articulation than explanation and more open.

Rossellini's method was a revolution in the cinema, called neo-realist, but unique to Rossellini. The other 'neo-realists' were naturalists, called *veristi* by Fellini, directors like Vittorio De Sica, Giuseppe De Santis.

The classical cinema is a cinema of homogeneity.

In it, difference is sutured, liaised, made to accord and join together. The *veristi* produced homogeneity and thereby belonged to the past.

Rossellini mapped out a future.

Rossellini's greatest early films were those with Ingrid Bergman. Rossellini used Ingrid Bergman in *Viaggio in Italia* where she played a northern European who has come to the Italian south where she is out of place. In *Stromboli*, Bergman played a sophisticated northern European refugee after the war who marries a simple Italian fisherman from the volcanic Sicilian island of Stromboli. They live in the primitive conditions of the island which the woman finds intolerable. In *Europa '51*, Bergman plays a spiritual figure in a materialist world.

Bergman was a Hollywood star out of true and place in these films. She is pure difference, a disturbance to what is. The films record the consequences of disruption and incompatibility, the heterogeneity of the real.

The film is impassive.

Rossellini's cinema is not a cinema of authenticity as is the cinema of De Sica. It is rather a cinema of what Rossellini called reality and truth.

The truth is founded on a *déliaison*. In a gap or tear in reality truth emerges.

In the monastery sequence of *Paisà*, the monastery is visited by three American chaplains. The monastery is simple, tranquil, an island of peace, protected from the war, far from the world. To enter the monastery is to pass into another place of strange beings as contrary to the world as Bergman would be.

The monks discover that one of the chaplains is Protestant, another Jewish. It is unthinkable to the monks, unimaginable and they are horrified.

They fall on their knees before the catastrophe, look to heaven, ring the bells.

The experience of the war by the monks is relatively indirect, matters of food shortages, small deprivations, distant noises. The American chaplains add exotic things from their knapsacks to the store of food: tinned milk, sardines, bars of chocolate.

The Americans are like invaders, occupiers, aliens, Jew and Protestant, the heresy of Luther, those who crucified Christ. They are like artillery shells and they wound. The Americans bring the scent of war to the monastery and more importantly they bring their difference.

The monks prepare a banquet for their guests.

The Americans are amused at the innocence of the monks, their inability to understand the ways of the world, their separation from it. The distress the monks feel on discovering a Jew and a Protestant is for the Americans a sign of simplicity and ignorance. The Americans think they know. It is their superiority.

At the banquet, the three chaplains are seated at the head table in the refectory. They are fed generously. The monks however will not eat. As a spoonful of soup is raised to the lips of the Catholic chaplain, he realises that his hosts are not eating and that they are regarding the Americans with silent compassion.

The monks tell them that they are fasting as a supplication to bring the wayward chaplains to the true faith. Their sacrifice is not a rebuke. It is an act of kindness and generosity.

At that moment the Americans are aware of a sacredness they had never known. They recognise for the first time in their lives where they are, what they do not know, what they might never know.

In 1948, Rossellini made *Il miracolo* based on a treatment by Fellini. In the film Anna Magnani plays 'Nanni' and Fellini is 'San Giuseppe'. They are the main characters. Nanni is a shepherdess tending her flock. She encounters a wanderer who seduces her (Fellini/San Giuseppe) then leaves her. Nanni is unaware or forgets what has happened. She becomes pregnant and imagines that the encounter she had had in the field was with (Saint) Joseph. She believes the birth she will soon experience is a holy birth and she a virgin.

She feels the sacred and awaits the miracle.

Nanni may be in error yet she is affected by something true and not simply about herself but about the world and its realities.

The world thinks her mad.

Fellini is not confrontational like Rossellini. His miraculous and sense of otherness is soft and gentle, not didactic. It requires only a shift of perspective to emerge. Fellinian miracles arrive by stealth.

The Rossellinian miracle alters the world.

Fellini also worked on the script of Rossellini's *Roma città aperta*, *Francesco giullare di Dio* and *Europa '51*. Fellini said: 'Rossellini est l'ancêtre duquel nous sommes tous descendus.' ('Rossellini is the forefather of us all.')

The late nineteenth-century actress Sarah Bernhardt was a close friend of the French novelist Pierre Loti. Loti wrote love stories in exotic settings. Loti's real name was Julien Viaud.

He joined the navy and in 1871 came to Tahiti, aged 21. There, he fell in love with a young Tahitian, called *Loti*, the name of a Polynesian flower. When he left Tahiti and *Loti*, he adopted her name as a *nom de plume*.

Bernhardt called Loti 'Pierrot le fou'.

It is fitting that 'Pierrot le fou', Godard's clown, reads out a passage from Élie Faure about the invisible that Velázquez painted, his ability to paint the air. Clowns are sensitive to these qualities as are masqueraders like Fellini and Loti.

The clown was a central figure for the European avant-gardes.

The cubed, multicoloured costume of the clown in Picasso's work disrupts the homogeneity of the surface of his paintings as the character of the clown disturbs the calm surface of fictions and reality.

SEE ALSO: CLOWNS, (THE) EYE, LOVE

Rubini 1

Intervista is composed of layers of films within films. In one of these, the actor Sergio Rubini plays a young journalist in the 1930s who takes the tram to Cinecittà to interview a beautiful blonde movie star.

Along the way he sees waterfalls, picturesque peasants, red indians and elephants.

Where do these come from?

On the tram, he meets a young girl, blonde and glowing, a luminous angel.

The scenes are organised by Fellini as if they are remembered by him and enacted by Rubini, his stand-in. Rubini is the young Fellini as he once was when he had gone to Cinecittà in the 1930s for the first time and on the way had met an angel … or so he suggests.

The presumed, invented memories are filmed as fragments, like real memory, including the persons, the supposed real Fellini.

La dolce vita: Maddalena and Marcello drive a prostitute home

The film is less a record of what is remembered than a film in which memory and identity are fabricated to appear not as memory or identity but as their fabrication, make-believe memory. The subject of the film is memory fabricated, illusions revealed.

Memories so filmed are neither true nor false.

Most, though not all Fellini films, are about memory. The characters in the films remember what you see or a narrator, as if he is Fellini, remembers and what he remembers and recounts is the film you see which Fellini off-screen is making as if it is the memory of another Fellini inside the film.

The act of remembering is a duplicate of an act of remembering in a different place.

The film you see in *Intervista* is the location of a film recording what you see. It is like the duplicate documentary of *I clowns* and *Prova d'orchestra* where the film doubles the documentary that is filming the circus and the rehearsal since the documentary is itself being filmed.

Fellini's documentaries are false in the sense of being staged but true because the staging is acknowledged.

All his films have this second order aspect hence his recourse after *La dolce vita* to artificial settings. No real settings would do for a subject which was artifice itself. If a sea was a real sea it would be a lie. Only as plastic would it be true ... and more fun.

The luminous vestal angel on the tram in *Intervista* is sublime while the movie star whom Rubini meets is vulgar and grotesque. Her beauty is over-stressed to the point of mocking itself, beauty taken too far.

Rubini, still young, is dazzled however by the experience.

What is that experience?

It is the experience of his dreams, the images he holds made into flesh, pink and voluptuous and wet. In effect he sees his dreams in a reality. The vocation of the movie star is to convince Rubini of her truth though Rubini has already convinced himself. He has created her, not reality. He is like Wanda who weaves her romantic white sheik of vulgar cloth in *Lo sceicco bianco* or Dottor Antonio who gives life to Anita on the billboard out of his desires. He tempts himself with her. She is only an image.

The encounter of Rubini and the diva is like that of Marcello (Marcello Mastroianni) and Sylvia (Anita Ekberg) in *La dolce vita* which turns Marcello's head as Rubini's head is turned from the vision of an ethereal angel toward an oversize earthly goddess, so stupendous, splendid and exaggeratingly fleshy as to seem as unreal as an angel and equally beyond grasp.

Marcello in *La dolce vita* is a stand-in for Fellini as Rubini is his stand-in in *Intervista*.

Marcello's name in *La dolce vita* is Marcello Rubini.

In *Intervista*, Mastroianni appears as himself, as the actor, in the disguise of the comic book character Mandrake the Magician. He is at Cinecittà playing Mandrake for an advertising film. In this costume he arrives unexpectedly like a magician might with a puff of smoke at Fellini's first floor office window at Cinecittà standing on a scaffold.

Cinecittà is where the film *Intervista* begins and where most of its action takes place. It is a film manufactured on a set whose setting is the film set. Two films side by side and similar are overlapped and intersected.

Intervista creates an imaginary space where films are being filmed. Filming films is the actual real function of Cinecittà. In Fellini's film it is included in his film, in fact is the central location of it, to function exactly like it normally functions, but doubled. Cinecittà is the place where films are made including a film that is set in Cinecittà where the film you are watching is being made and also has been made as if narrated and narrating in the same instant.

The studio in the film is real and false simultaneously. It is impossible to be sure of either state. This is Cinecittà. This is a make-believe memory of Cinecittà made in Cinecittà. It is images of images, remembered and brought to life as memory.

Where else could a Fellini film be made?

At Cinecittà, Fellini is filming Kafka's *Amerika* 'for' the film *Intervista* and that is seen 'within' the film *Intervista* which contains it like the doubling of *Otto e mezzo* within *Otto e mezzo*, two films at once. Fellini is not making a film of Kafka's *Amerika*, but pretending to make that film.

There is seldom a 'one' in Fellini's films without an 'other' to mirror it.

Cinecittà is also where a Japanese television crew in *Intervista* is making a film of Fellini making *Intervista* and where the filming by the Japanese crew is in turn being filmed by Fellini from another position outside *Intervista*.

Other films are also feigned as being made at the time on the Cinecittà lot.

After all, it is Cinecittà, isn't it?

In *Intervista*, Mastroianni, Fellini, Rubini, the crew of *Intervista* and the Japanese television crew drive out in a convoy of Mercedes to Anita Ekberg's villa near Frascati. They improbably lose their way and more improbably encounter a priest on a bicycle who knows exactly where Ekberg lives.

The actor–characters in *Intervista* play the characters of themselves in the scene. Fellini is Fellini, Mastroianni Mastroianni, Rubini Rubini, Ekberg Ekberg, and the film crew the film crew.

Everyone plays who they are and as a consequence who they are not because the play duplicates them.

Mastroianni, still dressed as Mandrake, waves a wand to unfurl a small screen in Ekberg's sitting room. He waves the wand again and on the screen is projected the Fontana di Trevi scene between Mastroianni and Ekberg (Marcello and Sylvia) from *La dolce vita* 27 years earlier.

The different times and incidents associated with these times play on other times and their events. Mastroianni and Ekberg watch themselves in a film of the present where they are actors as they were in the past in a film also as actors. Then they were characters, now they play themselves but are not by that fact less fictional or less divided or more true.

Godard was correct: documentary becomes fiction because reality becomes fiction in being represented and equally fiction becomes documentary because a film cannot help but reproduce what occurs.

The scene at Ekberg's house evokes decay, old age and death. To see Ekberg as young and beautiful is made poignant by seeing her old and blousy and it also makes her comic. Here fiction and documentary are side by side, in a zig-zag.

Decay and death are cruel jokes in Fellini's films: the funeral voyage of the
Gloria N, the absurd death of Augusto, the mock funeral in *I clowns* and
the clowns in real life, now old. Death is evoked in the scene because decay
is real enough (we are mortal) but against this reality is the fiction of images
which remains after the events filmed have passed but which film can resurrect in an image (images are not mortal).

The scene of Rubini with the movie star in her dressing room in *Intervista*
echoes the scene of Marcello enthralled with Sylvia in *La dolce vita*. It also
is an echo because Rubini is impersonating a young Fellini thus marking
out the ageing Fellini who projects himself in the young Rubini and who
observes his projection and his memories, feigned or real, from behind the
camera and on the set as the ageing Anita and the ageing Marcello observe
their young selves on the screen in *La dolce vita*.

The scenes and figures are caught up in images from which there is no
escape. On the screen Fellini is 'Fellini' and he is forever 'Fellini' and he
will be forever that 'Fellini' as he will no longer be the Fellini that he once
was.

In *E la nave va*, on the deck of the cardboard ship, gazing at the painted
sky and painted moon, one character remarks, 'It seems so real, as if it were
painted.'

Moraldo, in *I vitelloni*, leaves the seaside resort of Rimini and the restric-
ted horizon of the provinces for Rome, as Fellini had done. Moraldo too
knew an angel, the young boy who worked at the train station with whom
he chatted late at night and who waves goodbye to him as Moraldo departs
forever from a Rimini made in Ostia.

Moraldo is called Moraldo Rubini.

Marcello Rubini from *La dolce vita*, like the young man in *Roma* who plays
the young Fellini in another impersonation of Fellini, arrives in Rome from
the provinces. At the end of *I vitelloni* Moraldo Rubini departs from Rimini for the 'city'. He will arrive in Rome, slightly altered, with another name
and another face in another film.

The Rubinis and Fellinis are in a train of images where they circulate and metamorphose. Or each is like a facet of a gemstone which reflects and shimmers, constantly changing in reflected light.

Antonio Rubino was a comic strip artist when Fellini was growing up.

Rubino was the most famous, most poetic of all Italian comic strip artists at the time. His caricatures were naive, simple, direct.

The style of Rubino was refashioned by Fellini in his films. The ancestors of Fellini's films in circus, variety theatre, *fotoromanzi*, include the comic strip as graphic caricature, especially Rubino's comic strip.

The little people of Rubino's world were the model for the characters of *Giulietta degli spiriti*. Fellini showed the drawings of Rubino and those of Attilio Mussino, another cartoonist, to Piero Gherardi, his set and costume designer for *Giulietta*. He told Gherardi to give *Giulietta* the charm, *naïveté* and simplicity of Rubino's caricatures.

Giulietta degli spiriti is one of the least naturalistic of Fellini's films.

As in the archetypes of Borges, the model for the character Rubini is not Fellini but the archetype Fellini, not the person, but the image of the person made to seem in every respect like the person.

It is not accuracy Fellini seeks but deformation which is a way to emphasise not the object but the representation of it and in doing so allow it the freedom to migrate toward others rather than keeping it in the bounds of a single function.

It is the form of the thing that is important and forms, like grammar, are machines for the production of whatever utterances.

The archetype exists in a universe of archetypes without a beginning or an end. It can spin out toward other archetypes eternally, lock on to them for an instant, break off, return, reform, resettle.

The archetype lacks stability. Each example of it alters the entire series.

The pleasure of the archetype is its mobility in time and its perpetual passing. It is like an embrace of love, a memory sometimes even before it becomes an experience, or a memory already at the moment of being experienced, already felt as on the verge of disappearing and being gone, even though still warm and moist. Then, it is especially lost and poignant and you try in vain to cling onto it, to that moment that you have had which is passing forever.

Your memory is the clinging, the resurrection.

The lexicon deals in archetypes.

The shape of the Fellinian universe is round like the rings of the circus.

The 'i' at the end of a word in Italian pluralises.

Rubin(i) can be thought of as multiple versions of Rubin(o). I like to think it was Rubino who was the model for Rubinis belonging to the archetype Fellini.

He modelled his work on the work of Rubino, did he not?

SEE ALSO: CITATIONS, DOCUMENTARY, MARCELLO, RIMINI

Screen tests

There are two scenes in Fellini's films involving screen tests.

1. In *Otto e mezzo*, Guido, a film director, is trying to make a film. The location is near a spa hotel. Staying at the hotel are his wife, friends, mistress, producer, the actors, the crew, and his dreams and daydreams. The line separating the reality he lives and the imaginary he projects is unstable. What is subjective and objective wavers for him.

The film he seeks to make mirrors the life he is living but the reflections are distorted. Guido needs to enter his imagination fully in order to make his film but he is pulled back from it by the demands that surround him and by his own fears.

The whole of *Otto e mezzo* is a series of unsuccessful attempts by Guido to make the transition into his imaginary until at the end of the film the images of his memories and desires come to him and he can enter their world and hence the world he imagines that will be the world of his film.

The location for the film at the spa is a double one. It is the location for the film Guido is making and will make and of the film we are watching. The film we are watching, *Otto e mezzo*, will become the film Guido is to make, '*Otto e mezzo*'. These two halves of a film will become a single film.

In the course of preparing his film, Guido watches the rushes of screen tests for its various roles. The actors on-screen whom he watches in the tests impersonate characters amongst whom he lives off-screen and on whom his film will be/may be based.

The off-screen characters in *Otto e mezzo* accompany Guido into the viewing theatre to watch the screen tests. With his wife Luisa sitting by his side, they watch an actress playing Luisa and another playing his mistress Carla.

Earlier in the film Guido and Carla played out a scene together where she made believe that she had accidentally come to the wrong hotel room. It excited Guido immensely.

The scenes in the screen tests reenact scenes we have already viewed before of the 'real' mistress and the 'real' wife.

The mirror images have different times since what has been screened has not yet been filmed while at the same time what is unfolding has already unfolded and will unfold in a future. The resemblances between the film we watch and the one to be made, their doubled location, doubled characters, doubled actors, doubled times is not unlike the situation Mastorna is in when he discovers he is dead living in a world of the dead that is almost exactly like the world he was in when he was alive.

2. In *Intervista*, Fellini, like Guido, is making a film. The film is based on Kafka's *Amerika*. Preparing for it Fellini and his assistant try to find actors for the various roles. The actors sought play the roles of actors who are being sought. We watch a film within a film that resembles it whose subject, as with *Otto e mezzo*, is the making of a film. Thus the actors acting in the one film make believe they are actors in the other. In fact they are actors or they make believe they want to become actors whom they already are.

One method Fellini has for choosing actors in the film is to browse through an archive of photographs he keeps. These photographs of real persons are possible fictive characters. They are a catalogue of possibilities and of memories. Looking at a face it is possible to see an entire film. Browsing through these images is a way for Fellini to enter the world where the images are, a universe not of persons, but of the fancies they provoke. By means of these images, Fellini can pass to the world of film, can begin to enter his film as Guido does.

Guido, browsing through the characters of his life in his memory, begins to browse through his projected wishes and desires, begins to inhabit his own imagination. Thus, he too, like Fellini in the other film and like the Fellini he is the double for in *Otto e mezzo*, enters another world, a beyond of images where the characters in his film live as images and await him there and who, for most of *Otto e mezzo*, he cannot reach.

Every time Guido dreams, remembers and projects and thereby leaves the present world he is brought back to it by his wife, by his producer, by the needs of everyday and by his fears of what he imagines.

Other actors playing at being actors parade through Fellini's office in *Intervista* hoping that they will be chosen by Fellini to be characters to play actors which they already are and have already been chosen to be. As a consequence, Fellini's office is filled with lookalike actors wanting to impersonate lookalikes of themselves.

There is no position or person in the film or in most of Fellini's films which is not doubled. No one can help not wearing a mask and a costume and adopting manners and gestures which resemble them, the other of ourselves, our other half.

In *Intervista*, there is a scene of Fellini/'Fellini' shooting screen tests for the role of Brunelda in Fellini's Kafka adaptation. The actresses are blonde, excessively voluptuous and absurdly Teutonic, bathed by smooth, well-oiled, dark-haired young men, ridiculously Italian.

Rather than searching for originals to distort, the distortion is already there in the original, in the scene. But all this is faked, put into the scene. And yet …

If the spectacle on-screen for Fellini is a duplicate of another spectacle off-screen, it is because every off-screen presence for him, including his own, already contains the masquerade of itself as if a mirror is inside us making our reality virtual and our dreams the reality of an image we project, because our nature is divided.

Guido, for most of *Otto e mezzo*, cannot find the film he wants.

His difficulty is to discover a way to hold on to the images he finds in his memories and daydreams and to translate them into images in his film. The images live in an image world, elsewhere. Only if he can reach that elsewhere can he truly encounter them, be with them and hence be with himself. He has to leave where he is in order to arrive in the beyond where images live. This world, because it is filled with memories of what has passed, and desires of what is projected, is a world of the not yet living, to which Fellini must go and once there must literally restore these images, resurrect them, bring them to the surface, transform and hence save them. It is in that realm where film and poetry and spirits reside.

The trick is to come upon the mechanism of passage, like the mirror Orpheus gets hold of to pass through to the other world in Cocteau's *Orphée*.

Guido has a daydream of being master of a harem. The harem is a harem of all the women, past and present of his life, including his wife. They adore, celebrate, bathe, caress Guido, like so many mothers do an adored child. The harem has a temporal, regressive dimension: the infantile projections of an adult. The women flock around him and coo and he controls them, like a lion tamer, with a whip.

In reality, Guido's wife doubts him, suspects him of infidelity, may not love him and may leave him. In her anger and exasperation with him she is not unlike a mother. Guido goes all coy not unlike a little boy. He dreams of power and lives his impotence. In the daydream of the harem scene his wife is submissive, accepting.

He regains his power.

This scene is not exactly evidence of a Fellini theme or commentary about sexuality or on psychology or a discourse on sexual difference and middle-aged men, but a device of disproportion and mockery which is a means to accomplish the transition from where Fellini is into the images and film where he wishes to be.

These images are not exactly representations. They are magnifications, larger than reality, like the real world but on a different scale and belonging to different unlimited time, like the eternal Florence Mastorna visits in the land of the spirits when he is dead. This time is the same time of the photographs of actors that Fellini browses.

Magnification is Guido's Orphean mirror as it is Fellini's.

Guido's characters and his film have always been there from the beginning

waiting for him. All that was required was for him to be able to fully summon them up by detaching himself utterly from his life and giving himself
completely to his imagination.

At the end of the film he realises that he must pass to where they are,
where images are, in an elsewhere. And he finds them there being there
with them. His characters are dressed in white. They are like shadows, fantasms, shades of his mind. They hold hands and dance in a magic circle
into which Guido joyously enters, at last at one with his images and with
himself. His film is now possible and in this ending it begins.

A band of clowns plays circus music.

It is like the band that had greeted Cabiria, like Frou Frou's trumpet that
had responded to Bario, and like the angels of death dressed as peasants
who pass Augusto as he lays dying on the roadside.

The film we have been watching now ends as Guido enters it and the film
that he has sought to make commences. In that instant Guido and his characters who have always been present are effaced as the one film ends and
the other film begins.

Perhaps, when Bario and Frou Frou are wiped from the screen at the
end of *I clowns* it too is a beginning.

Perhaps all these moments at the end of Fellini's films are their beginnings.

In *La strada*, 'il matto' giggles happily, touched by a sense of the absurd,
when he first sees Gelsomina.

'What a funny face ... it looks like an artichoke.'

'Tu as un coeur d'artichaut', literally means, 'You have a heart like an
artichoke.' Figuratively it means, 'You give a little bit of your heart to everyone.'

SEE ALSO: EFFACEMENT, SPECTACLE

(The) Sheriff

Fellini founded a production company in the late 1950s in partnership with Rizzoli called *Federiz*. It was formed to produce the films of Fellini and encourage new talent. It succeeded only in producing Fellini's films. Soon after *Federiz* was formed Pasolini set out to make his first film, *Accattone*. He approached Fellini to produce it. Fellini turned him down. He thought the film too rough and raw.

Accattone is set in the Rome *borgate*.

The *borgate* were the slums of Rome on the periphery of the city, in part created as the consequence of an urban clearance in the 1930s by the Fascist state which dismembered and dislocated local communities near the Vatican and the Roman Forum. They were also a result of the postwar economic boom and internal migration to Rome from the Abruzzi and the Italian South.

The *borgate* were the consequences of modernisation and the forgotten leftovers of it.

Pasolini's characters were pimps, whores, thieves, a sub-proletariat. Pasolini briefly lived in the *borgate* when he arrived in Rome from Friuli in the early 1950s. He felt it to be an Eden, a world before the Fall, before the intrusions and corruption of the modernities of capitalism and development.

Pasolini idealised the socially-rejected and the socially-despised as spiritually pure because they represented for him pure difference. They stood out against a growing uniformity and functionalism. In the world being modernised they had no value, no use, no place. Their virtues for Pasolini were precisely in their desituation and rejection.

Pasolini found the slang of the *borgate* ancient and beautiful. Its survival, like the survival of Friuli, was the survival of an ancient world of difference

into the present, the light of difference for Pasolini, the beauty of difference. He learned Roman slang and transformed it into literary speech thus
shifting its function. In so doing he resurrected it. Roman slang is the language of two of his novels, *Ragazzi di vita* and *Una vita violenta*. Four of his
films are set in the *borgate*: *Accattone*, *Mamma Roma*, *La ricotta* and *La terra
vista dalla luna*.

The characters in *Accattone* have nicknames, like 'Accattone' ('Beggar' or
'Tramp'). One of them is called 'lo sceriffo'.
    The Rome *borgate* had names like Infernetto, Tiburtino III, Cessati Spiriti.
    Fellini found the *borgate* and its names suggestive and exotic. They
evoked a medieval China for him. Not Eden but a world dreamt by a child.
    Fellini hired Pasolini to advise him on the Roman dialect he wanted for
Le notti di Cabiria. Together at night the two of them wandered through
Infernetto and Tiburtino III.

Fellini was ill at ease in the *borgate* yet fascinated.
    He looked to Pasolini as a Virgil escorting him in Hell, or as a Geronte
transporting him there, or as a sheriff, protecting him. There were strange
beings in the *borgate* speaking a strange tongue. Pasolini was Fellini's adult
presence, his guardian.
    These roles are mythic and comic book ones.

For Pasolini the *borgate* was an Eden of reality, reality that had not been
demeaned, erased and debased by modernisation. Fellini, however, exaggerated the *borgate* as he wandered in it as he did for all realities he
encountered. 'Could this be Amazonia ?' he mused.
    The reality Pasolini found himself in was a film set for Fellini.
    For Pasolini the problem was to touch this reality to bring it close and
thus he reproduced it in his *borgate* films. Fellini thought differently. He distanced himself by magnifying it into the hyperbole and mockery of
Amazonia or the empire of China. The *borgate* of Fellini is evidently a stage
and a movie set.

From windows, from behind doors, out of dark alleyways in the *borgate*,

Fellini spied apparitions, darting little boys, appearing and vanishing: fantastic, wild, ancient beings.

They were like the figures in the shadowy streets of Venice in *Casanova*, or in the darkness of the labyrinth of ancient Rome in *Satyricon*, or the savage creatures in invented lurid locations on the studio set for *Roma*, especially its fantastic brothels. Or they were like the small children who escort the journalist through the corridors in *Agenzia matrimoniale*, and the deranged children who guide Gelsomina in *La strada*, or those called up by Guido's memories in *Otto e mezzo* which included Guido and perhaps also Fellini.

The Roman slang Cabiria speaks in *Le notti di Cabiria* may be accurate but it does not give her veracity. As a Roman whore she is absurd, laughable. Cabiria is a clown-whore, a whore-parody. Her language like her clothes ill suits her.

   The slang spoken by Pasolini's characters however is their truth and rightness.

   Everything about Cabiria and especially her language is disproportionate, out of true.

Side by side in the same place, Pasolini and Fellini were in different *borgate*. Each was the beloved character of the other in the world imagined by the other that each invented as necessary for themselves, as friends or lovers often do.

   Such misrecognitions are crucial for all amities.

   Pasolini was Fellini's 'lo sceriffo'.

Fellini sought Pasolini's advice for the final orgy (!) scene in *La dolce vita*.

> Thinking Pier Paolo Pasolini was an orgy expert, I invited him to supper one night. But Pier Paolo told me right away that he was sorry but that he knew nothing about bourgeois orgies and had never participated in one. 'Don't you know anyone who has?' I asked him.
>
>   No he didn't know anyone.

Perhaps it was not simply the roughness of *Accattone* that caused Fellini to turn Pasolini down.

Perhaps instead it was that the film was too true to life for Fellini to be believed, not close enough to Amazonia.

SEE ALSO: FELLINI

Spectacle

Fellini's films are filled with spectacles staged by the films as their central activity. Fellini is a master of ceremonies of spectacle.

There are three orders of spectacle: the field of professional spectacle; spectacles staged within everyday life; the spectacle of life itself.

In the area of the professional are the organised spectacles of variety theatre, television shows, the opera, the circus, cabaret, night clubs, dance, the fairground, fashion shows, the cinema, wrestling matches, theatre, parades.

Spectacles within everyday life include beauty contests, balls, religious festivals, strip-tease, carnival, dancing, street singing, fire-eating, masquerades, bonfires, weddings, the school play, a singing contest, charity shows.

I clowns: the circus performance

The spectacle of life involves the theatricalisation of the world. The most ordinary and banal activities can become theatre: evening promenades, sidewalk restaurants, the via Veneto, a bomb scare, parties, visits to whore houses, fucking, ice skating, spa baths, fencing, dinner parties, motorcycling, backstage, offices, the set.

These divisions are not clear in practice.

The spectacle of life is staged to seem more artificial than staged spectacles while in the circus or variety theatre there is no pretence at a mask. In reality, however, masks are worn but not acknowledged.

When Cabiria comes on stage at the variety theatre in *Le notti di Cabiria*, she is hypnotised by a magician dressed as the devil in a comic devil's hat with floppy horns. In a hypnotic trance, she reveals her true self to the audience, that is she reveals her desires for love and security. She gives a name to her dreamed-of true love: Oscar.

She is mortified that she has turned herself inside out in public. She waits until the theatre empties and then slips away. But outside someone is waiting for her. His name is Oscar … or so he says.

The meeting is the beginning of the game he plays with her of making her dreams come true in order to dupe her.

Oscar promises her marriage, true love, eternal happiness, security, devotion, all that she has longed for.

Her truth revealed in the theatre is falsified outside it.

Many of the most elaborate spectacles in Fellini's films are dream sequences. In them, the dreamer is dreamt. The subject is made an object. You dream of yourself. You tell the tale of yourself as hero, projecting yourself. The confusion often of a dream is the blur between speaking it and being spoken by it. Besides, there is no volition in a dream. You can't help yourself. The dream speaks you. And the dream is you.

The state of dream operates always in Fellini's films since he chooses characters who are dreamers and thus you can never tell whether the sight you see is objective or a projected dream.

Once reality is objectively gone, so too is the stability of appearances.

The truth of Cabiria is her secret dream and it is that secret that Oscar exploits unlike the journalist in *Agenzia matrimoniale* who tells Rosanna to go home and forget about marrying a werewolf.

The reason Augusto's final and deadly scam in *Il bidone* does not succeed is because it goes against rather than with the desires of his victims. It is difficult to make confidence tricksters believe a trick. There was no reason to believe him because their dream was the loot and the trick to get it.

Augusto, in losing his sense of theatre, loses his life.

Fellini would never do that.

It is play Fellini is after not your humiliation.

Play is an invitation for you to join the spectacle and to be in touch with your imagination which is the best part of you. That is the conclusion of *Cabiria*. When Cabiria is hurt and devastated at having been duped because of her needs and desires, Fellini holds out a hand to her of generosity, sympathy and acceptance, and tells her as the music of the young players on the road tell her and whom she joins that her dreams can be sustained in music, in play and the openness of spectacle and that is why Cabiria, for a brief second, at the end of the film, turns to the camera with a smile of recognition. She has won.

Oscar was no more than a force who could do nothing but steal and deceive. It was his nature. Oscar is a path of death and self-destruction. Cabiria (and Fellini) have better qualities and a better fate. They can adapt, they can change. In them is another spirit that wells up, that of life, when the band strikes up and strikes the force of their imagination.

For Fellini: 'The spectacle of the circus reveals the spectacles of the world and the truth of the mask uncovers the masks of reality.'

SEE ALSO: CONMEN (*BIDONISTI*), ILLUSIONISM

Spirits

Cabiria, in *Le notti di Cabiria*, lives a life where the objective and the subjective, the real and the spiritual, body and soul, inside and outside, are permeable.

Cabiria's desires, hopes, fears transfigure the world yet leave it unchanged. You see as she sees magical, wondrous elements that are part of its objectivity as if the world has a soul, especially when it is at its most drab. She senses that soul and makes it appear.

The ordinary becomes extraordinary, a delight, magical.

Cabiria finds possibilities where there seem to be none.

Though she is duped by her faith and has moments of doubt, her faith remains undiminished.

The world, even as it brings her to despair, renews her dreams. She has the capacity to respond and respond joyously, no matter what, and no matter how tinged the response is with sadness and melancholy and lamentation.

Cabiria can smile and cry at the same instant.

Otto e mezzo: the characters as spirits

The marvellous and spirituality are within the real she encounters and within herself enabling her to encounter it.

Gelsomina, in *La strada*, dies of grief and despair. Something beautiful dies within her with the death of 'Il matto'.

It is not only that 'Il matto', whom she loved, died, it is that something precious, indeed sacred, she had seen in the brutish Zampanò, who killed 'Il matto', also died and only she had seen it. That something was in the value of the pebble she wondered at in the moonlight, the tomato plant she sowed in a vacant field, the horse that passed her in the evening as she wept and the realisation of the preciousness of her insignificance and uselessness.

Gelsomina's despair and hopes leave a trace in a sad, sweet, mournful melody, the lament she first heard from 'Il matto', that she played on a toy trumpet, that she sang as if it was the voice of her soul singing.

These sounds came from inside and outside her, a spirit from within her and a spirit surrounding her.

One day, years after her disappearance, Zampanò, gruff, bestial, a lost soul, deaf to the universe, hears Gelsomina's melody on the road. He has just swallowed a whole ice cream cone in a single gulp. The lament is sung by a woman hanging out her washing. She tells Zampanò of Gelsomina's madness and of her death.

The melody and the memory touch Zampanò.

He drinks, becomes violent, aggressive, fights.

Late at night, bruised, sprawled on the beach, the sound of the waves before him, the sight of the heavens above him, he senses the immensity of the universe. He weeps at its fullness and emptiness.

These tears are the same tears Cabiria sheds on the verge of suicide.

Cabiria wipes her tears away at the sound of music to which her body starts to sway. She joins the players. She rediscovers her smile, looks shyly at the camera, and becomes a clown again. There never was another place for Cabiria.

Cabiria recalls Camilla in Renoir's *La Carosse d'or*. She gives up the golden coach, wealth, power, love, security to return to the other side, to the stage, to the mountebanks, acrobats, players, tumblers, clowns, Pierrots and Columbines. As she returns to a place made of nothing but these ephemeral shadows, the master of the troupe asks her if she will miss all that she has left behind.

'A little', she replies.

See also: Giulietta

Fellini made three films for television: *Block-notes di un regista*, *I clowns* and *Prova d'orchestra*. Television is the subject of *I clowns* and *Prova d'orchestra*. In both, a documentary film for television is being made (on the circus, on the orchestra).

Prova d'orchestra is a record of the false television film being made within it. The two films overlap. The exterior framing film shadows the interior television one. The film Fellini makes is a film not of the orchestra rehearsal (the subject of the television film), but of the filming of it (the activity of the television film).

These boundaries are by no means clear. You hear the voice of the interviewer (Fellini) who is directly addressed by the members of the orchestra, but you never see him nor the television crew. The orchestra players look right at the camera as they would in a real television interview. The shadow of the director (Fellini) is included in the shadowing of the one film by the other. The director and the film are both doubled.

The one true film is the documentary film that frames and presents the other documentary which is false. It is the documentary of falsity. But it too shares in the quality of falseness as all films must.

In *I clowns*, Fellini directs the film crew filming the clowns within the film and also directs the film which films the filming of the clowns. The border between the two films is porous. Fellini, depending on his position, is subject and object as he passes between films. In one incident, the clowns whose clowning he is filming within the film causes a bucket to land on his head, making him a clown. This act, staged as accidental, points to the other film which films it and makes Fellini more than a single identity in more than one place.

Block-notes di un regista is a television interview with Fellini. Also interviewed are Boratto, Masina, Mastroianni, Zapponi and others. The film was made for American television (NBC). Fellini wrote the script and directed the film in which he is the principal subject and player.

It is a self-portrait of sorts.

It is also, as with other films by Fellini made for television, a film about making a film for television.

There are scenes of mock television filming in other Fellini films: in *La dolce vita* (the false miracle), *Tre passi nel delirio* (the interview), *Roma* (an interview), *Ginger e Fred* (the television spectacular), *Intervista* (a Japanese television crew interview Fellini), *La voce della luna* (the moon is imprisoned on a gigantic television screen).

Such scenes follow a familiar Fellini pattern of staging. His films can be thought of as like variety theatre or the circus where 'numbers' are staged. The function of the film is not to be anything in itself except a setting to frame other spectacles and to point to its own activity of framing. The film is this setting into scene.

The structural function of the film is to display entertainments. The entertainments have little narrative motivation. The entertainments are not consequential or strictly narrativised. Their order is not necessarily dictated by the needs of a narrative logic but by considerations of tone, rhythm, rhyme, contrast and colour.

The loosening of narrative connectives in Fellini's films becomes evident after *Otto e mezzo* and liberates his images and their composition. His films become more open, more abstract, more spectacular.

The dance of Ginger and Fred staged for television is staged for the film which records both dance and staging. The delight of the scene is not simply the dance which television and the film are filming but the filming as part of the entertainment.

Television in Fellini's films is a citation of television, television abstracted as an image of it.

Citation points to the frame.

What is cited because it is a citation is doubly enunciated, once in having been represented and twice in that representation being cited. The frame is a further enunciating. It reveals what it cites as a discursive performance, a per-form-ance, the display of forms by turning the spectacle into a signifier.

Citation in film has another dimension.

There is a time gap in every image because the image records what is no longer and has passed. The image is the remnant of the passing. In that sense every image is a citation of a reality that has passed. To cite is to resurrect.

Fellini resurrects images, spectacles, what is already a representation, already an image and he does so by exaggerating the original.

Television is crucial for Fellini because of its pretence to truth (when it is false) and its pretence to the genuine (when it is vulgar). To reveal the grotesque of television is to call for something more pure and simple and for which Fellini is nostalgic. The force of the nostalgia requires the presence of television to see what is missing and is still valuable. Film is Fellini's instrument to mock television to reveal what it is by a caricature of it and to propose what might be by the display of the power of film.

See also: Citations

Television 2

Fellini accorded respect for television when it was close to the true. The true in television for him was the document and actuality. The forms he assigned to it were news, current affairs, interviews and investigative journalism.

When television entered into what Fellini called Art, which he associated with spectacle, fiction, narrative and masquerade, it seemed to him that it lacked the technical means to be artistic. At the same time it too often attempted to pass off its illusions as true using the capital it had accumulated of being direct and documentary. Television images at best for him had an illustrative quality not a creative one.

And as a medium to reproduce films, he loathed the miniaturisation, the blurred aspect of electronic emissions, the lack of clarity in the image.

And television gave the viewer too much power. The viewer could switch between channels, control the set, wander about, make a cup of coffee, talk on the telephone, be larger than the image quite different than the compulsion of the film image: grand, overwhelming and in darkness.

Fellini was into dream images of memory.

The television image it seemed to him lacked the power to captivate, enthral, transport you elsewhere. There was no magic.

The aesthetic possibilities of the television image were not explored by Fellini as they were by Antonioni, Rossellini, Marker, Rohmer and Godard. The distinction of film as art and television as communication (and vulgarity) holds only to a degree. It does not extend to what could be made of video techniques and has been made of them.

Digital has now altered everything.

For example, the experiments by Marker in image-construction and sound-image relations in *Level 5* and those by Rohmer involving the return of the film image by digital means to forms of painting in *L'Anglaise et le duc* where the narrative literally dissolves into the image and film becomes painting.

Video was experimented with by Antonioni in the mixing and manipulating of colour. It was experimented with by Rossellini in his search for the didactic, objective and duplicative image and by Marker and Godard in their juxtaposition and mix of techniques and forms of image-making (digital, video, film, painting, animation) and the juxtaposition of these with a range of techniques and forms of sound recording.

Godard worked with the full range of resources of video to superimpose, overlap, sketch, alter speed, scroll, change rhythms, play with colour and with the immediacy and spontaneity of filming in video and the ability to see its results instantaneously and refashion the image accordingly, capacities central to video and digital technologies. Video for Godard has initiated a revolution in editing and possibly in all the structures of film.

Television is not a technique but a means of diffusion. There is often a confusion in Fellini's statements between the two. The one may limit the other but only when it is brought into service to do so.

The relation is not a necessary one.

In *Prova d'orchestra* and in *I clowns* where there is a false television documentary filming and being internally filmed, there are splendid scenes of pandemic chaos. Such scenes were often staged by Fellini in relation to his framing of other spectacles like the circus, variety theatre and village fêtes.

In *I clowns* the disintegration into chaos occurs at the close of the mock clown funeral for the death of the Augusto Clown and by extension for the death of the circus. In *Prova d'orchestra* it is a consequence of the revolt of the orchestra musicians. The chaos in both instances and in other instances in other films becomes an abstract, kinetic and surface play of movement, colour and line.

It is a chaos of subject, clowns and musicians going wild, but not a chaos of forms. What is realised in the whirl of kinetic play is tactile, exhilarating.

It is pure energy.

Such energy specifies the cinema.

It is a disintegration of order as an opportunity to find something new which is a liberation and a possibility of new forms. This desire to unleash energy is one reason I think that Fellini's films are essentially comic and parodic, strategies that interrupt, disrupt, overturn, dismantle, and touch anarchy.

Antonioni's *Il mistero di Oberwald* used video mixing of colours to create images later transferred to celluloid. The screen explodes and dazzles with colour impossible to realise on film. Godard's *Histoire(s) du cinéma* uses video to juxtapose distant images that in combination ignite the screen.

These film/videos unleash an extraordinary vibrancy.

It may be that the opportunities offered by video were unseen by Fellini for the fact of television as diffusion. And it may have been also that the energy he valued only seemed possible in the cinema with its mystery, sensual enclosure and grandeur of scale.

Certainly, it did not offer him the play of deceit and artifice and games of illusion and magic that he believed only the cinema was capable of.

> Work for television? That means entering that ocean of blurred, confused images, into a hodge-podge that cancels itself out, a substitute for reality quantitatively as well as qualitatively. I have the unpleasant feeling of participating in a catastrophic flood of images, which television subjects us to every minute of the day and night. It wipes out more and more every shred of separation between the real and the visual and substitutes a kind of unreality to which our way of viewing had better get used to: two mirrors facing one another, duplicating themselves with infinite monotony and emptiness. It is not a question of style or of aesthetics. I don't even know what language to use for a television film.

There are infinite echos in the declaration.

One is the voyage to the end of neo-realism.

As Fellini reconstructed the via Veneto in *La dolce vita*, he reconstructed the television studio in *Ginger e Fred*, and the circus Big Top in *I clowns* but with the fabrication showing. Before the scene is filmed by Fellini it is refashioned to be filmed not to produce an illusion of reality but to display the refashioning of it.

Ginger–Amelia and Fred–Pippo are clowns. Ginger is a White Clown, orderly, bourgeois and sensible. Fred is an Augusto Clown, slovenly, anarchic and infantile.

Within the everyday is a secret make-believe, a complicit corruption of reality that the clown is contemptuous of, not respecting a false world pretending to be true. The clown exists above conformity and explodes its terms and illusions as shams.

Such destruction for Fellini is a precondition for creativity, a mixing of elements, a chance for new possibilities, a clearing of the ground.

The clown is who it says it is. Each aspect of the two sides of clowning are presented by Fellini as an interior state of ourselves exteriorised, one belonging to instinct and impulse, the other to reason and good sense. The truth, he says, is found imaginatively and creatively, by an act of artistry, not by deceit and false illusions.

Though Fellini's clowns, angels and innocents have a slight hue and tinge of the sacred, they bear a relation to the secular and social characters of Jean Renoir: the characters of the artist, the tramp, the poacher, the lover.

Fellini's clowns are their distant cousins.

Renoir's characters seek liberation from the socially banal and repressive by entering into the play of theatre. Such a social dimension is lacking in Fellini. The entry into make-believe has essentially transcendent and spiritual ends for him.

And yet the concern is not, by that token, without social implications.

When Ginger–Amelia and Fred–Pippo take the stage at the vulgar, indifferent television spectacular to dance the tap dance of their past and the past of dance and the past of the cinema, they transform the ugliness and superficiality of the television stage on which they find themselves by a perfect rendering of these pasts and a perfect rendering of the contraries of clowning which are, for a precious instant, as if by magic, in exact accord and harmony in their dance as happens in the trumpet dance and serenade of Bario and Frou Frou in *I clowns*.

Accompanied by the clowns Ginger and Fred in the midst of the horrors of television through which they navigate, the sublime is touched and another world sensed. As Ginger–Amelia and Fred–Pippo dance they go beyond the television stage into that other and precious world.

Their dance is a dance in cinema with the qualities of cinema: its luminosity and clarity and the grace of its movements, transcend, transform reality.

'We, in the East, look at life as if it was television, while you, in the West, look at television as if it was life.' (A Hindu sage)

The sage in the remark is a Fellini invention.

Trumpets

Gelsomina, in *La strada*, is taught by Zampanò to play the trumpet. She later plays the trombone while rehearsing an act with 'Il matto' ('the Fool').

The melancholy theme music associated with Gelsomina in the film is introduced by 'Il matto' on his violin. Gelsomina hears the music and is enraptured by it. It is later taken up by her on the trumpet.

The music transports Gelsomina to an elsewhere away from an everyday into a dreamlike, unreal realm compounded of her spirit and imagination. The trumpet music is pure enjoyment and enchantment. It is like the colour of images and the rhythm of their changes.

Sound in Fellini is not a support for reality and action. It is an essentially sensual dimension. In this dimension, logic and established discursive habits are weakened. Sound and vision take over to become their own reality. They stimulate and establish another reality, the reality of the senses.

The Gelsomina theme is not simply a theme, it is the very presence of Gelsomina. Thus, when Zampanò hears it being sung by the woman hanging out her washing and again hears it from inside himself or when he is on the beach from the outside of the universe reverberating inside of him, the hearing is a mixed sensation of fear, excitement, anxiety, desire. It is physical and a metamorphosis of physical states and emotional feelings.

Gelsomina is there, with him.

It is not precisely that the sound of the trumpet transforms the real and brings forward into it time and memory, but that the sound exists in the simultaneities of a past, inhabits the past and gives it presence. This is not story nor narrative. It is more concrete. It literally moves the world and encloses, embraces it.

It is the power of film.

The embrace is physical, warm, fluid and, I believe, maternal.

Fellinian memory is sensational.

The senses are shifters, images and sounds that transport/transform things into images and sounds.

Film establishes an autonomous realm of the sensual.

The music in Fellini's films is more than his stories require. This excess, which exceeds sense and function, is the essence of the stories. The film is not told so much as felt and physically so by hearing and seeing.

The hearing is less words than voices, less story than rhythm, less sense than tone. It is not narrative but narrative material: timbre, dissonance, harmony, simultaneity, discord, counterpoint, rhyme.

The excess and the materiality, the physicality of Fellini images, dismantles perspective, brings us close, creates disaccords, chaos, whirling and by so doing brings us toward the hallucinatory power of images no longer confined by sense.

In *La dolce vita*, the clown Polidor, played by the clown Polidor, performs a night club act with trumpet and balloons.

He plays a mournful melody on his trumpet. The melody is a lament like the lament of Gelsomina's theme. With it, Polidor summons a gaggle of balloons to the stage. When he exits, after his act of playing music of sadness and chagrin on his trumpet, he calls to the balloons with his lament and they follow him out as if they are living beings, as if the balloons, like Gelsomina's pebbles, have a soul.

The sounds of the trumpet make reality vibrate and in so doing refashion it.

The refashioning is a change of dimensions from one space with its time into another space with its time.

You move between levels.

The entirety of a Fellini film exists in this ambiguous space between what is there and not there, the visible and invisible, the comprehensible and the felt.

The appeal to the senses is a way to entice an audience to let go of one dimension, which is conventional, in order find the entrance to another which is marvellous, a passage from everyday into the cinema.

Fellini spoke of the cinema as woman, as circus, as regression. His cinema has qualities and scenes of confusion, simultaneity, chaos, babble, clanging and also moments of pure peace and silence, an exquisite beauty when everything is still and for an instant utterly empty; yet full thereby with expectation.

The oboist in *La voce della luna* makes the furniture in his room move when he finds and plays the mysterious 'infernal interval'. His oboe performs like Polidor's trumpet.

La voce della luna is a film about the transformation of the world into light, colour, voice, music.

The film quivers, scintillates, sparkles, sounds until it is possible to hear the voice of the moon and a voice from the bowels of the earth when the beyond becomes here and now and spirits and clowns descend.

Ivo Salvini is dazzled and enthralled.

Finally, there is the trumpet melancholy of Bario in *I clowns* that calls the clown Frou Frou from the dead. The two clowns, one of them present, the other not, play their trumpet duet. One trumpet comes from out of the past. The other enters into it from the present which is also Bario's future.

At this border, a border of time expressed as sound, the two clowns brush past each other for a precious instant, in eternity.

In that instant they are together while the gap that separates them endures.

Werewolf

In *Agenzia matrimoniale*, a journalist wants to do a story on the institution of the marriage bureau, a place of hope and despair, that is of fantasy. He seeks out a marriage bureau in a large Roman palazzo.

On a whim he concocts a story for the bureau that he is searching for a wife for his friend who has a particular illness: the friend, he says, is a werewolf. To his astonishment the bureau treats the request as nothing out of the ordinary. The next day he is telephoned by the bureau with an appointment to meet a young girl called Rosanna.

The journalist takes Rosanna for a drive in the country.

Rosanna is sweet, simple and desperate. She is emotionally desperate ('I form relations easily.') and economically desperate ('We are very poor.'). The werewolf, though howling at the moon, has attractions for her.

The journalist cannot continue with his joke.

He drives Rosanna back to Rome and advises her to look elsewhere. He is a trickster with a conscience.

The werewolf is a monster (and fictive). Rosanna is an innocent (and real).

The fictiveness of the werewolf is doubled in the film. He is constructed of words in the invented narrative of the journalist and he is also a vision that Rosanna can see. She sees him in the eye of her imagination stoked by her needs.

There is also another vision, another body: werewolves belong to history.

The journalist and tradition provide Rosanna with an image, like a film maker might, and her desires and needs do the rest: she projects herself into the image as if it were real, just like the cinema.

There is another strikingly monstrous couple in Fellini's world: Zampanò and Gelsomina. Zampanò, however, is real enough.

The combinatories, beauty and the beast, innocence and monstrousness, the real and the imaginary, have a history in literary and filmic representations: vampires, minotaurs, centaurs, King Kong, and in Cocteau's film, *La Belle et la Bête*.

The beasts evoke terror, desire, eroticism, and sometimes, tenderness by their vulnerability.

Murnau's vampire, suffering a sad loneliness and isolation, is endearing.

King Kong is emotionally fragile.

Cocteau's beast is shy and needy.

The beauties whom the monsters seek and seize are not without desire for the beasts. And we are not without desire for their desire.

Despite their (and our) screams of fear and protest, they (we) are excited, moved, often sentimentally touched at their plight of neediness in a beastly body.

Agenzia matrimoniale is an episode in a larger magazine film, *L'amore in città*, intended to present real situations with real persons playing themselves.

The Fellini episode parodies the assumptions of realism that inform the magazine. Everything is contrived in Fellini's episode. Nothing is taken from actual reality, none of the characters play anything but fictional characters, and the werewolf is an entirely concocted fantasy. The episode is based on the idea of what would happen in reality if you introduce into it an imaginary being. There are many films where this happens, where aliens arrive, or are constructed (Frankenstein), or someone takes a potion and becomes other than themselves (Jerry Lewis's *The Nutty Professor*, *Monkey Business*), or there are vampires.

It is the reverse of the narratives in *L'amore in città* which are intended to closely follow reality. The other exception is the Antonioni episode on suicide, *Tentato suicidio*.

Fellini, parodying the real by an openly-constructed mythical fantasy which is a lie, uncovers unseen real sentiments.

Beauty and beast stories are ancient.

Fellini's depiction of the couple, Zampanò–Gelsomina, is instructive.

Traditional monsters have a divided aspect, bestial and human. Beauty evokes the beast's humanity. The beast evokes in beauty her (and our) bestiality, at least not wholly innocent desires. And the beast also can evoke sentiments of sympathy as it does with Rosanna. The couple is composed of contraries, one the beauty, the other the beast, but it can also divide the characters of beauty and beast internally. The beast is in us and beauty is in the beast. The couple is the exacerbation of contraries hidden in the terms that constitute it.

Fellini combines a medieval beauty and beast tradition with a circus and clown tradition, the White Clown–Augusto Clown couple.

The clown couple functions like beauty and beast.

Each opposite is the other who brings out the otherness in the one.

Every Fellini film includes married couples or lovers, none of whom get on.

Some of the couples are central to his films. All are important. The couple is a variant of beauty and beast and White Clown–Augusto Clown. It is necessary that they be together and necessary that the relation be troubled. Each evokes desires in the other which are monstrous, impossible, scandalous yet unavoidable and delightful.

It crosses a boundary making the unthinkable a thought.

The situation is at the heart of Fellini's parodies and of the clowning about in his films, at once terrifying and touching. A perfect example is Wanda in *Lo sceicco bianco* in search of a white sheik who is only a character in a *fotoromanzo*. Her pursuit of this tawdry dream nearly destroys her new marriage. At the end of the film she returns penitent to her fearful, provincial little husband. She puts her arm in his and murmurs: ' … il mio sceicco bianco sei tu …' 'You are my white sheik.'

Fellini seemed obsessed by matrimony.

It is as if there is no choice.

This kind of reality simply does not go away.

SEE ALSO: ZOOLOGY

Zoology

Animals are present in all of Fellini's films.

In them are a camel, cats, chickens, a chimpanzee, cows, a crow, diomedes, dogs, donkeys, a duck, elephants, horses, lions, a monkey, a peacock, a rat, a rhinoceros, a seagull, sea monsters, a snail, a wolf, a werewolf.

Some of the animals are real. Others are made of cardboard, *papier mâché*, cloth. Some are merely referred to. Still others suggest only resemblances: the chopsticks in the hair of the French actress in *Otto e mezzo* recall an *escargot*; Anita in *I clowns* makes a face, shows her claws and roars like a tiger; Sylvia in *La dolce vita* howls like a dog; Frankie in *La dolce vita* cavorts like a chimpanzee.

Or a gorilla?

The place and function of animals are not uniform.

The appearance of some are naturally justified: a circus has lions, tigers,

La dolce vita: the monstrous fish on the beach

elephants and horses (*I clowns*); it is perfectly explicable that a rat might be in an old oratorio (*Prova d'orchestra*); it is not unusual for people to keep dogs (*Intervista*) or find stray cats (*Giulietta degli spiriti*, *La dolce vita*). These animal appearances are probable, mixed up with reality and the illusion of it as in a motivated narrative.

It is unusual even unlikely, however, that a camel should be on a beach outside Rome (*Lo sceicco bianco*) or a horse wander alone into town (*La strada*), or a cow appear from nowhere in the mist (*Amarcord*). These occurrences are not impossible. They are only relatively improbable, the more so by lacking narrative purpose and clear sense. Though they might occur, when they do they do not enhance a sense of reality. On the contrary, they raise questions about reality; are a cause to hesitate, a slight tear in the texture of the real.

In *E la nave va*, the hypnotised chickens, the seagull in the dining room, the rhinoceros in the hold are the least likely. Here, improbability enters. Though it could happen under some circumstances, essentially such events can only issue from the imagination.

Whether likely or not, motivated or not, all the animals in Fellini's films seem to be apparitions. They belong more to the fantastic than to the actual. They are like spirits and even angels. Animals can function in the films as a vehicle or instrument to take one elsewhere, to an implausible beyond, a shifter between worlds.

Animals help to create an atmosphere of magic in which metaphor and association are crucial elements.

Animals can accompany one into the fantastic.

Accepting them is to enter into another universe where unlikely appearances seem natural and the unlikely seems normal as happens in stories for children.

Children have a keen sense of the normalcy of the unreal.

The presence of animals in Fellini films recalls childhood and fairy tales. The animals exist where the wild things are.

The accompaniment into the fantastic can be direct and erotic.

Marcello in *La dolce vita* goes in search of milk just before dawn for Sylvia's kitten. They both purr, Sylvia and kitten. When Marcello finds the milk, he discovers Sylvia, all wet, in the Fontana di Trevi, her clothes clinging to her, amongst the gods in his fantasy dream. The milk for the kitten is forgotten. Sylvia is damp and inviting.

Sylvia is the source of milk with her full breasts. The event touches on the story of Juno creating the Milky Way told by Ivo in *La voce della luna*. Sylvia as Anita is the fantasy creature who gives milk in *Le tentazioni del Dottor Antonio*.

'Drink more milk, drink more milk.'

Giulietta, in *Giulietta degli spiriti*, brings Suzy back her cat which enables Giulietta to enter a world of sex and desire, fantasies and liberation.

Milk, a woman's sex, the eye – all these figure in Georges Bataille's Surrealist pornographic short poem-novel of 1928, *Histoire d'oeil*. It is also the subject of an untitled photograph by Hans Bellmer (1946), a saucer of milk, a vagina sitting in it, dripping milk like cum. The image comes directly from Bataille. In *Histoire d'oeil*, eye, vagina, egg, balls form an associative series which intersects with another of milk, urine, cum and tears, permitting unlikely and antithetical combinations.

By these means you may enter the fluidity and trance of dream and go to a beyond of images and characters.

Fellini admired the Surrealists, especially Buñuel: 'Buñuel is a larger-than-life author, incomparable.'

Animals are an intimate part of the fantastic. They can lead you to it, remind you of it, sustain you in it.

The peacock, who appears in the midst of the snow, amazes everyone in *Amarcord*. It is apparent that all that has been seen and will be seen, the whole of the film, the town, its events, its beings, including the peacock, could be apparitions, shadows from a dream, from an elsewhere and indeed they are.

If what is represented is what is imagined, the image is not a representation of what is but a projection of what might be, a procession of apparitions.

Three scenes:

In *E la nave va*, the Russian baritone sings to a chicken in the ship's galley to hypnotise it. Orlando, who is present at the scene in order to report it, is himself hypnotised and falls down in a faint.

Desire can normalise the incredible until it becomes the everyday. You begin to think the abnormal is perfectly standard.

In *Agenzia matrimoniale*, the journalist, in search of a wife for a friend he invents as a werewolf, seeks out a marriage bureau. He does not immediately find the marriage bureau which is in a large palazzo off Piazza Colonna in Rome. No one in the palazzo knows where the bureau is. He meets some children. They know. Giggling and dancing they accompany him.

The journey is through a labyrinth of corridors, floors and rooms. The journalist enters a magic world by way of children, the only creatures who have access to it. When he arrives at the bureau, he meets the owner of the bureau who is perfectly affable and resembles the devil.

In that world werewolves belong to the unremarkable.

The children would understand.

Who could all these people be in the marriage bureau? Where had they come from? Who had brought them there?

Children accompany you to another world.

In the hold of the liner, the *Gloria N*, there is a rhinoceros. No one on the ship ever quite knows what the rhinoceros is doing there. It is said, so said Fellini, that a rhinoceros in the hold of an ocean-going voyage is a usual feature.

The voyage is a funeral voyage to a mythical island. Because the voyage is metaphoric and mythical, explanations are essentially irrelevant.

The rhinoceros is a signifier lacking a referent.

He begins to stink badly. He is hauled up on deck in a sling on a crane where he is sprayed to cleanse him. He shits profusely. It is rumoured that he is ill, love-sick, the reason, it is said, for his stench and his refusal of food. Everyone on board is anxious to find reasons. The reporter Orlando is on the voyage precisely to provide explanations. Discovering very few, he invents many.

The *Gloria N* is fired upon by an Austro-Hungarian battle cruiser and goes down. Everyone is lost but the journalist Orlando. We see him rowing in a lifeboat. The rhinoceros is in the prow. Orlando remarks that the rhinoceros gives excellent milk. Presumably, the milk has saved Orlando.

Is the function of the rhinoceros then to give milk?

Is this what he represents?

I can't help thinking of 'Rosebud'.

Orlando's use of the milk of the rhinoceros as if to make the improbable possible only reveals the fullness of improbability assured by the vision of the rhinoceros rowed by Orlando in a lifeboat … and being filmed.

Who could Orlando be speaking to in the middle of a plastic sea with a sleeping cardboard rhinoceros by his side?

The entire voyage of the *Gloria N* is touched by similar improbabilities.

Above deck are the guests who intend to scatter the ashes of the opera singer Edmea Tetua, to pay homage to her person and to her sublime voice in a funeral ceremony on board with a chorus of voices. Edmea Tetua is present in the memory of the voyagers, by her recorded voice which is heard at her own funeral, in an old flickering film of her, in the arias being sung to her and by jealousies of the living for the dead who seem still within earshot.

Godard has remarked that we need to save the dead from the living.

Below deck is the apparently love-sick rhinoceros whose stench permeates the ship. The guests, devoted to Art, are petty, mean-spirited, jealous, false, perverse and competitive.

The only exception among them is a young girl, Dorotea, bathed in a heavenly light that accompanies her everywhere as if she has come from another world. She has the grace and innocence of an angel. Orlando is enthralled by her.

The other exception, the other figure of purity and sublimity, is found in shit, stink and ugliness. It is the rhinoceros of course.

The rhinoceros also is the young girl.
It [the rhinoceros] is in love and broken-hearted.

The rhinoceros belongs to the imaginary universe to which other Fellini animals belong and to which angels and clowns belong and where innocence is.

This is the reason those above deck cannot find a meaning for the presence of the rhinoceros and are not able to recognise the presence of an angel amongst them, nor accept the presence and physical immediacy of the dancing Serbs.

The sublime has no significance. It simply is and the fact of it is sufficient explanation. It is also a disruption as surely as a Rossellinian scandal.

Sublimity is where you least expect it.

The rhinoceros in the hold of the ship? But I put it there out of respect for the truth, in order to be faithful to the traditions of the sea. I was guaranteed that in those days, there was always a rhinoceros in every ship. It was obligatory for whatever voyage. It would be as if you asked me: '*Does this story take place on a ship? - Yes - And why is there a tiller on this boat?*' I can only answer: '*The tiller is part of the ship.*' Since I have been assured that in all sea voyages, a rhinoceros was necessary, I included a rhinoceros.

On the other hand, the rhinoceros is the better part of ourselves. He is the key to our survival.

Does he not save Orlando?

Nietzsche compared the horn of the rhinoceros to Christianity. Once it had a function but it had one no longer and no one knew what the horn of the rhinoceros once served.

Well, some say it is an aphrodisiac.

SEE ALSO: CLOWNS, WEREWOLF

Bibliography

This brief selective bibliography consists of works that I found of particular interest in preparing the book. Of these, the most interesting were by Barthélémy Amengual, André Bazin, Pascal Bonitzer, Alberto Moravia and Pier Paolo Pasolini.

I was also stimulated by the essays written by Mireille Latil-Dantec, Christian Metz and Sylvie Pierre.

The remarks concerning Fellini in Gilles Deleuze's book are extremely suggestive.

Abruzzese, Alberto, 'Giulietta degli spiriti,' Occhio Critico, no. 1, January–February 1960, pp. 32–4 (for the statements by Sadoul and Moravia)

Amengual, Barthélémy, 'Itinéraire de Fellini: du spectacle au spectaculaire' in 'Federico Fellini: 8½' special number of Études Cinématographiques, nos 28–9, Winter 1963, pp. 3–26

———, 'Fin d'itinéraire: du "côté de chez Lumière" au "côté de Méliès"', Études Cinématographiques, nos 127–30, 1981, pp. 82–108

———, 'Une mythologie fertile: "Mamma Puttana"', Positif, no. 322, December 1987, pp. 26–8

———, 'Propositions pour un portrait du jeune Fellini en néo-réaliste', Positif, nos 413–4, July/August 1995, pp. 6–11

Assayas, Olivier, 'Sic Transit Gloria N', Cahiers du cinéma, no. 355, January 1984

Bachmann, Gideon, 'Federico Fellini: "The Cinema Seen as a Woman"', Film Quarterly, vol. 34 no. 2, Winter 1980/81, pp. 2–9

Baldelli, Pio, 'Fellini e la storia "interna" della narrativa' in Pio Baldelli, Film e opera letteraria (Padua: Marsilio, 1964), pp. 380–404

———, 'Dilatazione visionaria del documento e nostalgia della madre chiesa in Fellini' in Pio Baldelli, Cinema dell'ambiguità (Rome: Samonà e Savelli, 1969)

Bazin, André, Qu'est-ce que le cinéma?, vol. IV (Paris: Éditions du Cerf, 1962), pp. 122–8, 129–33, 134–42, 143–5, 146–9

Betti, Liliana and Gianfranco Angelucci (eds), Casanova rendez-vous con Federico Fellini (Milan: Bompiani, 1975)

Bondanella, Peter, The Cinema of Federico Fellini (Princeton: Princeton University Press, 1992)

——— (ed.), Federico Fellini: Essays in Criticism (New York: Oxford University Press, 1978)

Bonitzer, Pascal, 'Memoire de l'oeil (Amarcord)', Cahiers du cinéma, nos 251–2, July/August 1974, p. 75

————, 'Casanova', *Cahiers du cinéma*, no. 275, April 1977

————, '*La cité des femmes*', *Cahiers du cinéma*, no. 318, December 1980

————, 'Le rhinocéros et la voix', *Cahiers du cinéma*, no. 356, February 1984

————, 'La cité dolente', *Cahiers du cinéma*, no. 381, March 1986

Cahiers du cinéma, 'Enquête sur Hollywood', *Cahiers du cinéma*, no. 54, Christmas 1955

Calvino, Italo, 'La parola alla difesa', *La Repubblica*, 24 November 1983

Ciment, Gilles (ed.), *Federico Fellini* (Paris: Éditions Rivages, 1988)

Cirio, Rita, *Il mestiere di regista: intervista con Federico Fellini* (Milan: Garzanti, 1994)

Curchod, Olivier, 'Le sourire et la fresque *le Satyricon*', *Positif*, no. 276, February 1984, pp. 31–7

Deleuze, Gilles, *Cinéma 2, L'Image-temps* (Paris: Les Éditions de Minuit, 1985)

Fantuzzi, Virgilio, 'Controlettura del *Casanova*', *La Civiltà Cattolica*, no. 3053, 3 September 1977

————, *Cinema sacro e profano* (Rome: La Civiltà Cattolica, 1983)

————, *Il vero Fellini* (Rome: Ave Editrice-La Civiltà Cattolica, 1994)

Farassino, Alberto, 'Provare e inutile l'orchestra non c'è più', *La Repubblica*, 15 March 1979

Fellini, Federico, 'Registi davanti alla TV (Federico Fellini)', *Cinema Nuovo*, no. 134, July/August 1958, pp. 59–61

————, 'Témoignages (André Bazin)', *Cahiers du cinéma*, no. 91, January 1959

————, 'La ricerca della verità', *Filmcritica*, vol. XI no. 94, February 1960

————, 'Confessione in pubblico', *Bianco e nero*, no. 4, April 1963, pp. 1–20

————, 'Lettre à Alberto Grimaldi sur un projet de film et dessins' (1970), *Positif*, nos 200–2, December/January 1977–8

————, 'Fellini' in Tay Garnett, *Portraits de cinéastes: Un siècle de Cinéma* (Paris: 5 Continents Hatier, 1981), pp. 105–12

————, *Fare un film* (Turin: Einaudi, 1993)

————, 'Federico Fellini' in Adriano Aprà and Stefania Parigi (eds), *Moravia al/nel cinema* (Rome: Associazione Fondo Alberto Moravia, 1993), pp. 103–16

Fieschi. Jean-André, 'Cabiria trépanée' *Cahiers du cinéma*, no. 174, January 1966, pp. 77–8

Fofi, Goffredo and Gianni Volpi, 'Entretien avec Federico Fellini', *Positif*, no. 409, March 1995

Ginzburg, Natalia, '*Amarcord*', *Corriere della Sera*, 10 February 1974

————, 'Un mondo stregato', *La Stampa*, 28 September 1969

Grazzini, Giovanni (ed.), *Federico Fellini: Comments on Film* (Fresno: California State University, 1988)

Jousse, Thierry, 'La fée électricité', *Cahiers du cinéma*, nos 431–2, May 1990

Kast, Pierre, 'En termes de fable: Entretien', *Cahiers du cinéma*, no. 164, March 1965

Kezich, Tullio, 'L'intervista lunga' in Federico Fellini, *Giulietta degli spiriti*, ed. Tullio Kezich (Bologna: Cappelli, 1965)

———, 'Fellinpoli e una nave che va, non non sa dov'é', *La Repubblica*, 21 December 1982

———, *Fellini* (Rizzoli: Milano, 1988)

Latil-Dantec, Mireille, 'Le monde du cirque et le monde comme cirque: *Les clowns*', *Études Cinématographiques*, nos 127–30, 1981, pp. 52–64

Metz, Christian, 'La construction "en abyme" dans *Huit et demi, de* Fellini', *Essais sur la signification au cinéma*, vol. 1 (Paris: Éditions Klincksieck, 1971), pp. 223–8

Monti, Raffaele, *Bottega Fellini* (Roma: De Luca Editore, 1981)

Moravia, Alberto, 'Roma prende la cicuta', *L'Espresso*, 24 August 1969, pp. 12–13

———, '*L'Intervista*', *L'Espresso*, 1 November 1987

Pasolini, Pier Paolo, 'Nota su *Le notti*' in Federico Fellini, *"Le notti di Cabiria" di Federico Fellini*, ed. Lino Del Fra (Bologna: Cappelli, 1957)

———, 'L'irrazionalismo cattolico di Fellini' (1960), *Con Pier Paolo Pasolini*, ed. Enrico Magrelli (Rome: Bulzoni, 1977)

Pieri, Françoise and Aldo Tassone, 'Entretien avec Federico Fellini (*Amarcord*)', *Image et Son*, no. 284, May 1974, pp. 59–67

———, 'Aux sources d'*Amarcord*: Les récits felliniens du *Marc'Aurelio*', *Études Cinématographiques*, nos 127–30, 1981, pp. 19–33

———, 'Federico Fellini, écrivain au *Marc'Aurelio*', *Positif*, nos 244–5, July/August 1981, pp. 22–32

Pierre, Sylvie, 'L'homme aux clowns',

Cahiers du cinéma, no. 229, May/June 1971, pp. 48–52

Scalfari, Eugenio, 'Con il Maestro parlando di donne', *La Repubblica*, 17 July 1979, p. 13

Tassone, Aldo, 'Entretien avec Federico Fellini', *Positif*, no. 181, May 1976, pp. 6–11

———, 'Entretien avec Federico Fellini', *Positif*, no. 182, June 1976, pp. 34–42

Tornabuoni, Lietta, 'Fellini: Cinecittà o niente', *La Stampa*, 28 December 1986, p. 3

Verdone, Mario, *Federico Fellini* (Rome: Il Castoro, 1994)

Viviani, Christian, 'Les sunlights de Fellini et les feux du music hall', *Études Cinématographiques*, nos 127–30, 1981, pp. 37–46

Volta, Ornella, 'Huit entretiens autour du *Casanova* de Fellini', *Positif*, no. 191, March 1977, pp. 6–15

———, 'Le film que Fellini ne tourne pas' in Gilles Ciment (ed.), *Federico Fellini* (Paris: Édition Rivages, 1988)

Zand, Nicole, 'Mauvaise conscience d'une conscience chrétienne', *Études Cinématographiques*, nos 28–9, Winter 1963

Zanelli, Dario, 'Dal pianeta di Roma' in Dario Zanelli (ed.), *'Fellini Satyricon' di Federico Fellini* (Bologna: Cappelli, 1969)

Zanzotto, Andrea, '*E la nave va*', *Trafic*, no. 12, Autumn 1994

Zapponi, Bernardino, 'Roma & Fellini' in Bernardino Zapponi (ed.), *Roma* (Bologna: Cappelli, 1972)

———, *Il mio Fellini* (Venice: Marsilio, 1995)

Filmography

The films listed have all been directed by Fellini. Fellini shared the direction of *Luci del varietà* with Alberto Lattuada. *Agenzia matrimoniale*, *Le tentazioni del Dottor Antonio* and *Toby Dammit* were episodes within longer films whose other episodes were directed by other film-makers.

LUCI DEL VARIETÀ (1950)
d: Alberto Lattuada, Federico Fellini
p: Alberto Lattuada, Federico Fellini
sc: Federico Fellini, Alberto Lattuada,
Tullio Pinelli, Ennio Flaiano *asst d*:
Angelo D'Allessandro *c*: Otello Martelli
ed: Mario Bonotti *set/cos*: Aldo Buzzi
mus: Felice Lattuada.
lp: Carla Del Poggio (*Liliana*), Peppino
De Filippo (*Checco*), Giulietta Masina
(*Melina Amour*). 100 mins.

LO SCEICCO BIANCO (1952)
p: Luigi Rovere *st*: Federico Fellini, Tullio
Pinelli, Michelangelo Antonioni *sc*:
Federico Fellini, Tullio Pinelli, Ennio
Flaiano *asst d*: Stefano Ubezio *c*: Antonio
Belviso *set*: Raffaelo Tolfo *mus*: Nino
Rota.
lp: Alberto Sordi (*Fernando Rivoli*),
Brunella Bovo (*Wanda*), Leopoldo
Trieste (*Ivan Cavalli*), Giulietta Masina
(*Cabiria*). 85 mins.

I VITELLONI (1953)
p: Luigi Giacosi *st*: Federico Fellini,
Tullio Pinelli, Ennio Flaiano *sc*:
Federico Fellini, Ennio Flaiano *c*:
Roberto Gerardi, Franco Villa *set*:

Mario Chiari *ed*: Rolando Benedetti
mus: Nino Rota.
lp: Franco Interlenghi (*Moraldo*), Alberto
Sordi (*Alberto*), Franco Fabrizi (*Fausto*),
Leopoldo Trieste (*Leopoldo*), Riccardo
Fellini (*Riccardo*), Eleonora Ruffo
(*Sandrina*), Carolo Romano (*Michele*),
Lida Baarova (*Giulia*). 103 mins.

AGENZIA MATRIMONIALE (1953)
p: Cesare Zavattini *st*: Federico Fellini *sc*:
Federico Fellini, Tullio Pinelli *asst d*:
Luigi Vanzi *c*: Gianni Di Venanzo *set*:
Gianni Polidori *ed*: Eraldo da Roma *mus*:
Mario Nascimbeni.
lp: Antonio Cifariello (*giornalista*), Livia
Venturini (*la ragazza*). 18 mins.

LA STRADA (1954)
p: Dino De Laurentiis, Carlo Ponti
st: Federico Fellini, Tullio Pinelli *sc*:
Federico Fellini, Tullio Pinelli, Ennio
Flaiano *asst d*: Moraldo Rossi *c*: Roberto
Gerardi, Franco Villa *set*: Mario Ravasco
ed: Leo Catozzo *mus*: Nino Rota.
lp: Giulietta Masina (*Gelsomina*),
Anthony Quinn (*Zampanò*), Richard
Basehart (*Il matto*). 94 mins.

IL BIDONE (1955)
p: Giuseppe Colizzi st: Federico Fellini,
Ennio Flaiano, Tullio Pinelli sc: Federico
Fellini, Tullio Pinelli, Ennio Flaiano asst
d: Moraldo Rossi c: Otello Martelli
set/cos: Dario Cecchi ed: Mario
Serandrei, Giuseppe Vari mus: Nino
Rota.
lp: Broderick Crawford (Augusto),
Richard Basehart (Picasso), Franco
Fabrizi (Roberto), Giulietta Masina (Iris).
104 mins.

LE NOTTI DI CABIRIA (1957)
p: Dino De Laurentiis st: Federico
Fellini, Ennio Flaiano, Tullio Pinelli sc:
Federico Fellini, Tullio Pinelli, Ennio
Flaiano asst d: Moraldo Rossi,
Dominique Delouche c: Aldo Tonti
set/cos: Piero Gherardi ed: Leo Catozzo
mus: Nino Rota.
lp: Giulietta Masina (Cabiria), François
Périer (Oscar), Franca Marzi (Wanda),
Dorian Gray (Jessy), Amedeo Nazzari
(Alberto Lazzari), Polidor (the monk).
110 mins.

LA DOLCE VITA (1960)
p: Giuseppe Amato st: Federico Fellini,
Ennio Flaiano, Tullio Pinelli sc: Federico
Fellini, Tullio Pinelli, Ennio Flaiano asst d:
Guidarino Guidi, Paolo Nuzzi, Dominique
Delouche c: Otello Martelli set/cos: Piero
Gherardi ed: Leo Catozzo mus: Nino Rota.
lp: Marcello Mastroianni (Marcello),
Walter Santesso (Paparazzo), Anouk
Aimée (Maddalena), Yvonne Furneaux

(Emma), Anita Ekberg (Sylvia), Lex
Barker (Robert), Adriano Celentano
(rock and roll singer), Alain Cuny
(Steiner), Polidor (night-club clown),
Magali Noël (Fanny), Laura Betti
(Laura). 178 mins.

LE TENTAZIONI DEL DOTTOR ANTONIO
(1962)
p: Carlo Ponti st: Federico Fellini sc:
Federico Fellini, Tullio Pinelli, Ennio
Flaiano, Brunello Rondi, Goffredo Parise
c: Otello Martelli set/cos: Piero Gherardi
ed: Leo Catozzo mus: Nino Rota.
lp: Peppino De Filippo (il Dottor
Antonio), Anita Ekberg (the woman on
the billboard). 60 mins.

OTTO E MEZZO (1963)
p: Federico Fellini, Angelo Rizzoli st:
Federico Fellini, Ennio Flaiano sc:
Federico Fellini, Tullio Pinelli, Ennio
Flaiano, Brunello Rondi asst d:
Guidarino Guidi, Giulio Paradiso,
Francesco Aluigi c: Gianni Di Venanzo
set/cos: Piero Gherardi ed: Leo Catozzo
mus: Nino Rota.
lp: Marcello Mastroianni (Guido), Anouk
Aimée (Luisa), Sandra Milo (Carla),
Claudia Cardinale (Claudia), Edra Gale
(Saraghina), Mario Pisu (Mezzabotta),
Polidor (clown), Caterina Boratto
(woman at the spa), Annibale Ninchi
(Guido's father), Giuditta Rissone
(Guido's mother). 114 mins.

GIULIETTA DEGLI SPIRITI (1965)
p: Angelo Rizzoli *st*: Federico Fellini,
Tullio Pinelli *sc*: Federico Fellini, Tullio
Pinelli, Ennio Flaiano *asst d*: Francesco
Aluigi, Liliana Betti, Rosalba Zavoli *c*:
Gianni Di Venanzo *set/cos*: Piero Gherardi
ed: Ruggero Mastroianni *mus*: Nino Rota.
lp: Giulietta Masina (*Giulietta*), Mario
Pisu (*Giorgio*), Sandra Milo (*Susy, Iris,
Fanny*), Valentina Cortese (*Valentina*),
Caterina Boratto (*Giulietta's mother*),
Sylva Koscina (*Sylva*), José de Villalonga
(*José*). 129 mins.

TOBY DAMMIT (1968)
p: Alberto Grimaldi, Raymond Eger *st*:
Edgar Allan Poe: *Don't Bet the Devil
Your Head sc*: Federico Fellini,
Bernardino Zapponi *asst d*: Francesco
Aluigi, Eschilio Tarquini, Liliana Betti *c*:
Giuseppe Rotunno *set/cos*: Piero Tossi *ed*:
Ruggero Mastroianni *mus*: Nino Rota.
lp: Terence Stamp (*Toby Dammit*), Salvo
Randone (*Padre Spagna*), Polidor (*an old
actor*). 37 mins.

BLOCK-NOTES DI UN REGISTA (1969)
p: Peter Goldfarb (NBC) *st*: Federico
Fellini, Bernardino Zapponi *sc*: Federico
Fellini, Bernardino Zapponi *asst d*:
Maurizio Mien, Liliana Betti *c*: Pasquale
De Santis *ed*: Ruggero Mastroianni *mus*:
Nino Rota.
lp: Federico Fellini, Giulietta Masina,
Marcello Mastroianni, Caterina Boratto,
Bernardino Zapponi. 60 mins.

FELLINI-SATYRICON (1969)
p: Alberto Grimaldi *st*: Petronius:
Satyricon sc: Federico Fellini, Bernardino
Zapponi *asst d*: Maurizio Mien *c*:
Giuseppe Rotunno *set/cos*: Danilo
Donati, Luigi Scaccianoce *ed*: Ruggero
Mastroianni *mus*: Nino Rota.
lp: Martin Potter (*Encolpio*), Hiram
Keller (*Ascilto*), Max Born (*Gitone*),
Salvo Randone (*Eumolpo*), Mario
Romagnoli (*Trimalcione*), Magali Noël
(*Fortunata*), Alain Cuny (*Lica*), Fanfulla
(*Vernacchio*), Lucia Bosé (*the
noblewoman who suicides*). 138 mins.

I CLOWNS (1970)
p: Elio Scardamaglia, Ugo Guerra *st/sc*:
Federico Fellini, Bernardino Zapponi
asst d: Maurizio Mien *c*: Dario Di Palma
set/cos: Renato Gronchi *ed*: Ruggero
Mastroianni *mus*: Nino Rota.
lp: Professional clowns playing
themselves. 93 mins.

ROMA (1972)
p: Lamberto Pippia *st/sc*: Federico Fellini,
Bernardino Zapponi *asst d*: Maurizio
Mien *c*: Giuseppe Rotunno *set/cos*:
Danilo Donati *ed*: Ruggero Mastroianni
mus: Nino Rota.
lp: Peter Gonzales (*Fellini at 18*),
Federico Fellini, Marcello Mastroianni,
Anna Magnani, Gore Vidal, Alberto
Sordi. 119 mins.

AMARCORD (1973)

p: Franco Cristaldi *st/sc*: Federico Fellini, Tonino Guerra *asst d*: Maurizio Mien *c*: Giuseppe Rotunno *set/cos*: Danilo Donati *ed*: Ruggero Mastroianni *mus*: Nino Rota.

lp: Bruno Zanin (*Titta*), Puppella Maggio (*Miranda*), Armando Brancia (*Aurelio*), Stefano Proietti (*Oliva*), Ciccio Ingrassia (*Teo*), Magali Noël ('*Gradisca*'), Maria Antonietta Belluzzi (*the tobacconist*), Josiane Tanzili ('*Volpina*'). 127 mins.

IL CASANOVA DI FEDERICO FELLINI (1976)

p: Alberto Grimaldi *st*: Giacomo Casanova: *Storie della mia vita sc*: Federico Fellini, Bernardino Zapponi *asst d*: Maurizio Mien, Liliana Betti, Gerald Morin *c*: Giuseppe Rotunno *set/cos*: Danilo Donati, Luigi Scaccianoce *ed*: Ruggero Mastroianni *mus*: Nino Rota.

lp: Donald Sutherland (*Casanova*). 170 mins.

PROVA D'ORCHESTRA (1979)

p: Alberto Grimaldi *st/sc*: Federico Fellini, Brunello Rondi *asst d*: Maurizio Mien *c*: Giuseppe Rotunno *sets*: Dante Ferretti *ed*: Ruggero Mastroianni *mus*: Nino Rota.

lp: Baldwin Bass (*the conductor*), Federico Fellini, Franco Mazzieri (*trumpet*), Clara Colosimo (*harpist*), Elisabeth Labi (*pianist*), David Mauhsell (*first violin*), Claudio Ciocca (trade unionist). 70 mins.

LA CITTÀ DELLE DONNE (1980)

p: Franco Rossellini *st/sc*: Federico Fellini, Bernardino Zapponi, Brunello Rondi *asst d*: Maurizio Mien *c*: Giuseppe Rotunno *set*: Dante Ferretti *ed*: Ruggero Mastroianni *mus*: Luis Bacalov.

lp: Marcello Mastroianni (*Snàporaz*), Anna Prucnal (*his wife*), Ettore Manni (*Katzone*), Iole Silvani, Donatella Damiani, Fiametta Barailla, Silvana Fusacchia, Sylvie Mayer. 145 mins.

E LA NAVE VA (1983)

p: Franco Cristaldi *st/sc*: Federico Fellini, Tonino Guerra *asst d*: Giovanni Arduino *c*: Giuseppe Rotunno *set*: Dante Ferretti *ed*: Ruggero Mastroianni *mus*: Gianfranco Plenizio.

lp: Freddie Jones (*Orlando*), Barbara Jefford (*Ildebranda Cuffari*), Victor Poletti (*Aureliano Fuciletto*), Peter Cellier (*Sir Reginald Dongby*), Norma West (*Lady Violet Dongby*), Pina Bausch (*La Principessa Lherimia*), Janet Suzman (*Edmea Tetua*). 132 mins.

GINGER E FRED (1985)

p: Alberto Grimaldi *st*: Federico Fellini, Tonino Guerra *sc*: Federico Fellini, Tonino Guerra, Tullio Pinelli *asst*: Gianni Arduini *c*: Tonino Delli Colli, Ennio Guarnieri *set*: Dante Ferretti *cos*: Danilo Donati *ed*: Nino Baragli, Ugu De Rossi, Ruggero Mastroianni *mus*: Nicola Piovani.

lp: Giulietta Masina (*Amelia–Ginger*), Marcello Mastroianni (Pippo–Fred), Franco Fabrizi (*television presenter*). 125 mins.

INTERVISTA (1987)

p: Pietro Notarianni *st/sc*: Federico Fellini, Gianfranco Angelluci *asst d*: Maurizio Mien *c*: Tonino Delli Colli *set/cos*: Danilo Donati *ed*: Nino Baragli *mus*: Nicola Piovani.

lp: Federico Fellini, Maurizio Mien, Anita Ekberg, Marcello Mastroianni, Sergio Rubini (*journalist*), Pietro Notarianni (*Fascist official*). 113 mins.

LA VOCE DELLA LUNA (1990)

p: Mario and Vittorio Cecchi Gori *st*: Ermanno Cavazzoni: *Il poema dei lunatici sc*: Federico Fellini, Tullio Pinelli, Ermanno Cavazzoni *asst d*: Gianni Arduini *c*: Tonino Delli Colli *set*: Dante Ferretti *cos*: Maurizio Millenotti *ed*: Nino Baragli *mus*: Nicola Piovani.

lp: Roberto Benigni (*Ivo Salvini*), Paolo Villaggio (*Il prefetto Gonella*), Nadia Ottaviani (*Aldina*), Marisa Tomasi (*Marisa*), Syusy Blady (*Aldina's sister*), Sim (*the oboist*). 118 mins.